MATRIX MANAGEMENT SUCCESS

Method *Not* Magic

By

Ronald A. Gunn
Strategic Futures® Consulting Group, Inc.

ISBN 0-7414-4129-2

Published by:

INFINITY
PUBLISHING.COM

1094 New DeHaven Street, Suite 100
West Conshohocken, PA 19428-2713
Info@buybooksontheweb.com
www.buybooksontheweb.com
Toll-free (877) BUY BOOK
Local Phone (610) 941-9999
Fax (610) 941-9959

Printed in the United States of America

Printed on Recycled Paper

Published September 2007

DEDICATION & ACKNOWLEDGEMENTS

This book is dedicated to Alexandra Gunn and Marietta Gunn – each daughter unique, each daughter wonderful – and to Grace Gunn, great mother, great friend.

Thanks to Jennifer Thompson, President of Strategic Futures Consulting Group, Inc. who ushered this book from airy concept to concrete completion; it simply would not have happened without her. Thanks also to Ellen Goodwin for the cover, Ken Cofield for the graphics, and Erika Fitzpatrick for helping translate my thoughts into English. Any shortcomings in readability are strictly my own. A tip of the hat to two splendid mentors -- Edwin T. Crego, Jr. and Karl Albrecht. Last but certainly not least, I thank all of my clients. I learn something new and valuable every time I work with them.

FOREWORD

Changes in communication and project-management technology have greatly increased the ease with which matrix management can be applied successfully. Advancements in communications in the past 50 years, and new, more transparent work planning, budgeting, and execution systems, have largely removed the obstacles that once stymied effective matrix management.

The key remaining barriers to success in matrix management are more human in nature. Many enterprises reorganize from time to time, and often do so with a few charts, a set of revised mission/function statements, and an all-hands meeting or two. Unclear roles, relationships, and rules of engagement can and do confound the best-laid plans. The move to matrix management requires more than these measures, in part because the roles and rules are often foreign and require changes in behavior and shifts in culture.

In a nutshell, effective matrix management implementation requires a careful, not a careless or disorganized, approach. I have written this book based on matrix management consulting, coaching, facilitation, and training experience with more than three dozen clients, mostly private corporations, but also with several agencies of the U.S. government. The purpose is to alert thoughtful executives, other members of management, and organizational development (OD) practitioners to the issues, strategies, and tactics that are important to success.

I benefited from an excellent orientation to matrix management provided by Dr. Daniel Roman, of the Graduate School of Business at The George Washington University in Washington, D.C. Dr. Roman learned matrix management in the aerospace industry – arguably the original source of matrix management more than a half-century ago. In my work over the past 20 years, I have built upon Dr. Roman's foundation, and listened to my clients – their knowledge, their issues, their challenges – to refine the solutions that lead to success. I thank all of these people for the ideas that readers find useful, and accept responsibility for any advice that is less helpful.

INTRODUCTION

Nearly a half-century ago, social theorist Harold Garfinkel struggled to understand society using unconventional means. Why? He had dismissed conventional approaches as ineffective. Calling himself an ethnomethodologist, he adopted the premise that the only way to understand a social group is to disrupt it – to glean reality's fleeting essence as a previously stable social situation shatters. His argument is that to understand how something works, take it apart – perhaps shake it apart – and then put it back together again.

In one of his many experiments to understand social reality, Mr. Garfinkel loaded cages of several dozen live chickens onto a flatbed truck, drove to a crowded urban park at lunchtime, and let the chickens loose in the middle of an unsuspecting crowd so he could study social behavior in the midst of chaos. Who turns to whom to make sense of this unusual occurrence? Who turns to whom for help? Who asserts themselves to restore order and how is order restored? What kind of power and influence is used?

This notion of forcing understanding through disruption can often be a byproduct of many a corporate reorganization, if we are open to learning.

Seeing the way individuals and institutions respond to matrix management is clearest when it is applied to a specific organization, or even a particular industry. When it comes to our discussion of matrix management, abstract discussions of generic situations won't do – we need a specific town square on which to release the chickens! Therefore, I will talk about matrix management in the context of a wide range of organizations and industries, both private and public, so there is an applicable lesson for almost every circumstance.

This book is for readers interested in exploring options for organizational structure that are different from traditional hierarchies. You may already be carrying around some mental images of what matrix management is and how it works. Chances are your mental model of matrix management works for you intellectually. However, it's possible that you have come up against some frustrations and organizational roadblocks because other people are using a mental model that is different from yours.

But it is important to remember that the way an organization works – or is supposed to work – is most clear at the very top of the organization. Things literally and figuratively go downhill from there and tend to become foggier at lower levels.

Let me tell you about an experience that illuminates this point. I once participated in the design and fielding of a survey to top executives in the federal government, whose purpose was to discern emerging trends so that training programs could anticipate demand rather than react to training needs after they had already crested. One of the most telling survey findings related to the relative difficulty of implementing strategic change. At the very highest levels of the federal government, individuals were largely unanimous that strategic change was not an area of great challenge. However, individuals representing progressively lower levels of the executive service reported more difficulty in adopting strategic change.

It is clear that executives who are conversing with like-minded peers can underestimate the challenges of implementation felt by lower-level staff members. Executives whose ideas for change are pronounced from on high – and are divorced from the grinding concerns of how to carry it out at all levels of the organization – likely will be disappointed in the results. Executives are mistaken if they believe that a few well-chosen remarks will cause genuine change.

Matrix management requires careful rather than careless implementation. This seems obvious, but my first-hand experience has taught me the importance of emphasizing this point. Matrix management is more than a concept or a "state of mind," although it is both of these. Achieving clarity at all affected levels of the organization takes old-fashioned hard work.

When people have differing images of an organizational structure, and of its roles and its rules, they find that it is very difficult to get things to work correctly. I liken it to "playing bridge in an insane asylum," where each patient plays by his own peculiar set of rules. The problem is in distinguishing *activity* from *results*. Each patient appears to be playing the game, but how will we know when there is a winner, or even when the game is over?

Matrix management, or any form of management for that matter, works best when the roles and rules are widely understood. I hasten to add that these roles and rules should not be defined at such a microscopic level of detail that there are no degrees of freedom or opportunities for growth and change. However, the level of understanding should be sufficiently defined so that the organization does not have to discover each day's rules anew.

This book seeks to redress the relative paucity of useful literature concerning matrix management. The best stuff is no longer in print; I was lucky enough to be exposed to some of it by one of my most cherished management professors a quarter-century ago. The more intricate (and decidedly less sexy) management approaches that were honed in engineering and other research and development (R&D) environments a half-century ago don't garner much interest from many of today's business book publishers.

Matrix management doesn't rely on magic or mysticism or the fluff of the month. This approach is for the hard-driving, high-producing organization willing to institute disciplined, methodical change. That alone may explain why it suffers from a less-than-burning popularity. If your organization is ill positioned for such a challenge, you may want to lobby for a slower, simpler, or less powerful approach in your organization. On the other hand, if you believe that matrix management can serve as a springboard to a more dynamic, agile, and cross-functional enterprise, then I hope this book helps you achieve the progress that you seek and deserve.

CONTENTS

CHAPTER 1

Matrix Management: *Method, Not Magic*

Why Matrix Management Now?

A county government executive from Nevada e-mailed me to say that her traditional hierarchical reporting system wasn't working as her organization moved toward multidisciplinary projects and an increasing number of public-private partnerships. "We need more effective communication and action across the organization, not just within the functional areas," she said. Her message sums up the basis for the growing interest in the power of matrix management – where multiple multidisciplinary teams pursue shared objectives using shared resources.

Employees who are "boundary spanners"– people who are "in the know" about what is going on throughout the organization – have always been the backbone of cross-organizational collaboration. These sociable personalities gain extraordinary access to information and insights. The more introverted among us rely directly or indirectly on these garrulous folks to be the human bridge to cross-organizational collaboration.

Boundary spanning is much easier today than it was in the past. Technology helps us span boundaries more effectively and rapidly through Web-enabled processes, instant messaging, e-mail, and cellular technology of one kind of another. Tom Friedman's book, *The World is Flat*, (New York: Farrar, Straus and Giroux, 2005) tells the story of how we have shortened the distances between individuals, organizational components, organizations, and nations. On the other hand, even with technological advantages, or, perhaps, because of these technological advantages, it is no longer enough to rely upon our gregarious colleagues to figure out if the right hand knows what the left hand is doing. Boundary spanning needs to be less an accident of personality and more an intentional outcome of an interwoven organizational structure that mirrors today's networking technologies.

Many companies and government agencies are striving toward integration and the one-organization concept as a matter of conscious choice rather than happy accident. They are doing their utmost to manage relative scarcity of talent, infrastructure, and financial resources – resources outstripped by incessant demand imposed by more pending projects than wherewithal – with minimal disruption, and maximum agility and productivity. They are focusing on high-impact goals, increasing their speed, attaining powerful abilities to solve complex problems, and promoting creativity and organizational learning throughout. They are seeking to make the highest and best use of all assets – human, financial, and infrastructural. Achieving these results requires cross-organizational collaboration, a greater degree of sophistication, and a willingness to share resources to avoid waste. It requires pulling together toward common goals rather than pulling apart in schoolyard-style shoving matches.

Organizational "silos" and the habits of thought and behavior that accompany silos too often stand in the way of cross-cutting collaboration. Today's speed of business and the multidisciplinary problems that we are trying to solve leave most traditional hierarchies out of breath. People may move quickly but their organizations frequently struggle to keep up, resulting in staff frustration and fatigue. It's like trying to solve digital problems with analog technology. As organizations take more multidisciplinary approaches to accomplishing work – many times virtually or through strategic alliances – matrix management presents a more viable option to traditional methods.

The sporadic formation and disbanding of cross-functional teams for a project does not constitute a matrix organization. Some people tell me that their organization has always operated on an informal matrix basis, where staff from different functions work together in cross-functional teams. Cross-functional teams are the building blocks of the matrix organization. Participation on such teams gives staff valuable experience in spanning boundaries and working with others from outside their discipline toward a shared goal using shared resources but it does not unleash the full potential power of your horizontal organization.

Indeed, more and more people in organizations are working on increasing numbers of multidisciplinary, or cross-functional, teams. When only a few such teams are operating at once, things are relatively manageable. However, a tricky dynamic gets unleashed when a significant number of resource-consuming cross-functional teams start competing with one another for talent, money, and infrastructure. In addition, when employees begin relating to one another vertically, horizontally, and diagonally, effective communication is even more difficult.

The network approach has expanded beyond the world of computers and cyberspace to the way we think about human organization. Dee Hock, author of *Birth of the Chaordic Age* and other works, coined the term "adhocracies," in referring to new organizations where the relative absence of hierarchy and the fast connections permit the organization to get its work done in an agile way. The matrix affords more structure, role definition, and a set of rules for making decisions, allocating resources, and accomplishing tasks, and is an expression of a networked, rather than a rigidly hierarchical, way of doing things. Like our information technology systems, which rely on partners, alliances, and outsourcing, matrix management is a networked approach with defined roles, rules, and tools.

Organizations choose the matrix structure for one or more of the following reasons:

- **Goal focus** – improving the organization's ability to accomplish high-impact goals;

- **Customer focus** – improving the organization's ability to anticipate and surpass customer expectations;

- **Speed** – reducing the amount of time to accomplish cross-functional objectives;

- **Ability to handle complexity** – improving the ability to solve complex problems;

- **Capacity utilization** – ensuring the highest-and-best use of all human, financial, and infrastructural assets, such as equipment, plants, computers, fleet, etc.; and

- **Creativity and organization learning** – mixing disciplines and staff from diverse backgrounds to cultivate new thinking and to expand technical depth and breadth.

Here are some other specific potential advantages to matrix management:

- A reduction in the number of organizational levels, resulting in a flattened hierarchy

- An elimination of unnecessary work that fails to add value to the enterprise, particularly "coordinative" and "checkers-checking-checkers" kind of work

- An organization design based on processes that add genuine value, such as product development or order entry, rather than functions or departments that may become process-obsessed or narcissistic

- A structure that brings focus and power to the management of change as well as expands agility

- The use of management horizontally and diagonally so that the "white spaces" between traditional vertical lines are both managed and bridged. Organizational boundaries are reduced over time, resulting in economies as core processes are performed more efficiently and effectively

- Greater professional-development opportunities afforded by meaningful interaction with other disciplines

- Greater self-management and a wider job "wingspan," or spectrum of work performed by jobs in the organization

- Higher and better use of staff time and talent

- Stark illumination of resource constraints with a corresponding requirement to set priorities in an explicit way

- More rapid team-based elimination of work that fails to add value to the enterprise.

If some or all of these benefits are sufficiently motivating, you may wish to design and implement a matrix organization. This book will give you some concepts and tools to use on the way. However, be forewarned: The matrix cannot be "wished" into place. "Drive-by management" won't make it happen either. The hard work of defining and negotiating how this structure should work simply cannot be avoided. Then, and only then, can the process of learning how to derive matrix management's powerful benefits be pursued with lasting success.

The "matrix management" concept is not always fully understood. Some people talk about matrix management as "dotted-line relationships," but, if you'll notice, these folks rarely talk about what's truly involved with a dotted-line relationship. Other people refer to matrix management as being "where one division loans out its employees to another division or to a project." While each of these responses contains a grain of truth, neither tells the whole story.

Differing or unclear definitions of matrix management impede implementation success. Clarity is essential. Remember, organizational clarity is greatest at the top. So . if you are at or near the top of your organization and things are unclear to you... well, you know the rest of the story. When an organizational change occurs, employees promptly ask, "What am I supposed to do differently?" Without clarity, that question won't be answered and, as a result, employees will conclude that the French are right after all: "The more things change the more they remain the same."

So before our conversation about matrix management can begin in earnest, a glossary of terms is needed. We need to define the essential terms that permit us to think and talk about matrix management using a standard vocabulary; the objective of this chapter is to set forth this glossary. These terms have strong implications for how best to proceed when designing and implementing a matrix organization. There's more to it than merely "declaring" that you have a matrix organization. Success is about method, not magic. This chapter defines the matrix organization, and benefits to adopting matrix management.

What is a Matrix?

Webster's defines a matrix as "something within which something else originates or develops." How does this apply to matrix management? It applies in the sense that the matrix itself matters less than the multidisciplinary processes that *develop in and from* the matrix. *Webster's* goes on to describe a matrix as "something resembling a mathematical matrix, especially in its rectangular arrangement of elements into rows and columns."

Rows and columns, the horizontal and the vertical. The horizontal and the vertical intersecting in a grid, where the grid is a network of interfaces.

While *Webster's* definition of matrix takes us part of the way, my working definition of a matrix organization takes things the rest of the way. As shown in the diagram below, it is an organization where ***cross-functional teams are cobbled together in a network of interfaces, and where the teams pursue shared objectives using shared resources with a defined set of roles, rules, and tools.***

Diagram of a Matrix

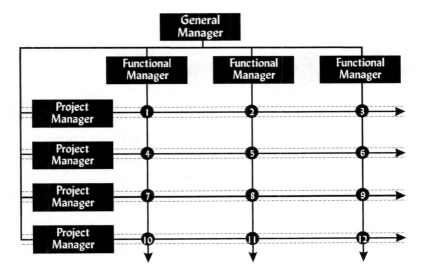

(Note: While the horizontal manager is depicted as "project manager," in this diagram, other possibilities include goal manager, product manager, customer or customer segment manager, process manager or other alternatives based on the organizing principles behind your matrix.)

The vertical lines of the matrix organization are most similar to the traditional hierarchy. Throughout this book, we use the term vertical leader, functional leader, and vertical function to refer to traditional organization departments, such as marketing, sales, finance, R&D, engineering, manufacturing, and so forth. Everyone is accustomed to traditional vertical (hierarchical) management. Most of us are hard-wired to think "up the chain": What do the bosses above us want and how shall we organize our efforts to please and provide? The hierarchical model has been around since humans organized for military action. Matrix management, on the other hand, has been around for less than a century, having been introduced in the 1940s. Matrix management has a ways to go before it becomes "second nature."

In the traditional hierarchical method of setting tasks, shown below, vertical managers call the shots regarding nearly all aspects of the work, with the top set of bullets most related to "doing the right things," and the bottom set of bullets most related to "doing things right":

- ❑ What is to be done?
- ❑ When will it be done? "**doing the right things**"
- ❑ Why is it being done?
- ❑ How much money is available to do it?
- ❑ How well has the total effort been done?

Plus...

- ❑ How will it be done?
- ❑ Where will it be done? "**doing things right**"
- ❑ Who will get it done?
- ❑ How well has our input been integrated into cross-cutting efforts?

In a matrix organization, the manager in the vertical chain is still calling shots, but not all of the shots: The difference is that power is shared throughout the enterprise. In the matrix array of power **horizontal matrix teams** have responsibility and authority related to the first five bullets – what, when, why, how much, and how well – while the **vertical chain** retains responsibility and authority for the final four bullets – how, where, who, and how well. This arrangement is called the ***Basic Matrix Role Dichotomy***, or more commonly, the "role splitter." The arrangement of distinct matrix responsibilities and authority is a central and inescapable component of successful matrix management.

Matrix management does not erase the vertical hierarchy. However, non-traditional **horizontal management** becomes *as* important, and sometimes *more* important, than the traditional vertical hierarchy, depending on the issue at hand. Matrix management is "both/and" rather than "either/or." This arrangement is unfamiliar, counter-intuitive, and status-threatening, particularly to those who are accustomed to all-or-nothing thinking, which posits – mistakenly – that if organizational power is not all vertical, then it must be all horizontal, rather than both.

Horizontal management refers to management of a multidisciplinary matrix team toward a defined purpose. (More about matrix teams later in this chapter.) A horizontal team may be organized on the basis of a project, which is the first and most familiar basis for a matrix organization, but increasingly, matrix organizations are comprised of teams that are organized according to the following categories:

- ❏ Customer
- ❏ Geography
- ❏ Product
- ❏ Business Line (e.g., residential vs. commercial)
- ❏ End-to-End Process
- ❏ Goal

The horizontal matrix team is comprised of members who are drawn from each participating function. These members are located at the **matrix interface.** The

matrix interface — there are 12 interfaces in circles numbered 1 through 12 depicted in the matrix organization chart shown in the previous diagram — is where matrix authority and responsibility come into play, largely determining how horizontal and vertical priorities are reconciled. As we will see in subsequent chapters, the matrix interface is a real person — a "go-to person," a "key individual," a "vertical liaison" — who really makes or breaks the matrix organization. Despite its importance, this position is most often neglected or staffed carelessly. Inadequate staffing of the matrix interface will result in matrix failure.

The concept itself is simple: think horizontal, think vertical, think interface. While the *concept* may be clear enough, the "devil-is-in-the-details" *implementation* challenges bring on the migraine headaches.

Roles, Responsibility, and Authority in Matrix Management

The first challenge that most people confront in matrix management is confusion about roles, responsibility, and authority. They ask a legitimate question: "How can one person possibly report to two bosses?" This *appears* to violate the **unity of command** principle that is inherent in the matrix organization, which states that one should receive orders from only one individual in the chain of command.

The unity of command management principle is a good one that has survived through the decades. I believe in it and will stick with it albeit in a different configuration. In a well-managed matrix, the violation of the unity of command principle is *apparent,* not real. This apparent violation can be avoided using the **Basic Matrix Role Dichotomy**, or the "role splitter," which, quite simply, divides the basic management responsibilities to ensure that there is separate accountability and power, without overlap. It sets up the structure so that functional management divisions along the vertical axis, such as marketing, finance, and engineering, define how the task will be done and who will do it. The vertical governs "talent" and "technique."

The horizontal responsibilities and prerogatives address team or process-management questions, such as what, when, why, budget, and evaluation. The successful matrix is "both/and" rather than "either/or," i.e., both the horizontal and the vertical are balanced and aligned. In later chapters, you'll learn the difficult process of fine-tuning the vertical and the horizontal in matrix management.

One of the most common reasons why matrix organizations fail and why matrix management suffers a bad reputation in some people's eyes is that the Basic Matrix Role Dichotomy isn't put into place or, even worse, is given lip service by vertical managers, who are in reality continuing their previous habits, persisting in "calling all of the shots."

Without clear roles and rules of engagement, organizational "gridlock" occurs, resulting in a lack of clarity as to who is initiating, who is deciding, and who is doing. In these circumstances, the matrix degenerates quickly into personnel politics and power plays. Politics are always at work in an organization because resources are rarely, if ever, unlimited. There's nothing inherently wrong with "politics." But if the matrix lacks an explicit, rational foundation provided by the Basic Matrix Role Dichotomy, then the politics – the human way of solving problems and allocating resources when rational means don't work – become unbridled and the system dysfunctional.

I recall a situation where the President and CEO of a NASDAQ-traded company – a visionary executive with several advanced degrees – called together the company staff and announced the move to "matrix management." He drew some circles on the flip chart, talked a bit about a "one-firm concept" of operating and achieving goals that cut across the entire organization. After his 15-minute presentation, he asked if there were any questions. Hearing none, he declared, "You see, they understand it." In fact, the opposite was true: The staff didn't understand enough of what was being said to ask any questions at all!

An essential part of organizational design and implementation planning is to map out the arrangements that will be used in managing the enterprise. All too often this mapping is given short shrift. Magically, somehow, people are supposed to "know what to do," and then "just do it!" Well, they don't know and they can't do what they don't know.

Another requirement is that matrix players must have a clear sense of the goals, objectives, and performance metrics. If there is inherent conflict or excessive competition among managers' goals, objectives, and performance expectations, then the cooperation required to share resources won't develop. Stated differently, there must be both vertical and horizontal alignment of goals, objectives, and metrics if the matrix is to function properly. Unhealthy competition or conflict can create gridlock in the matrix — across functions, across locations, and throughout the organization. Constructive tension is good. Destructive tension is bad.

Parenthetically, some top executives favor "Darwinian Management," which consists of unleashing a flurry of initiatives, projects and/or priorities that exceed the organization's capabilities and capacities to deliver with the idea that "survival of the fittest" will prevail. Apart from costs to clarity, productivity, and morale, this approach may work appropriately in some traditional hierarchical organizations as a leadership strategy for purging feeble concepts and players from the enterprise. However, it is simply a bad idea in a matrix organization because it distorts the alignment of objectives with commensurate resources and tends to promote destructive tension.

Ironically, while matrix management requires collaboration and "sharing," it rests upon the unspoken assumption that there is strong leadership at the top that is committed to the matrix management way. "Sharing" does not mean that staff are shared "50-50" or "60-40" or any other "tug-of-war" distribution of their time and accountability. Top management needs to have the courage to make the structural shifts that are defined by the Basic Matrix Role Dichotomy. Absent that courage and the structural shifts that are required in defining horizontal and vertical roles, staff will be caught in the middle and some of the most common maladies and complaints concerning matrix management will surely ensue.

The legacy power in any organization is with the vertical chain. Vertical managers give the training, mentoring, awards, promotions, and perks to create goodwill and loyalty among employees who report to them in the traditional supervisor-supervisee relationship. More than these professional and personal bonds, however, are the budgeting and financial tracking systems that are organized on the basis of the vertical hierarchy. Human resource policies, procedures, and forms have been developed on the basis of the traditional hierarchy. As the matrix organization is introduced, the horizontal team is typically underpowered. It takes awhile before the constructive tension between the horizontal and the vertical can be cultivated and used to its full advantage. Top leaders may need to temporarily and artificially boost the power of the horizontal matrix teams and their leaders to move this process along.

When top leaders insist that everyone follow the roles and rules of the new matrix organization, the pain of change will surely make itself known. I have seen top-level, high-status vertical leaders go to the CEO or COO seeking approval for decisions about issues relative to a particular customer only to be told firmly and directly that this decision is now the matrix team leader's call. These words are very difficult for the vertical leader to hear and accept. Why? Because that leader, who under the previous traditional hierarchy was instrumental in developing and maintaining the customer relationship, is being told to step aside for the good of the matrix system. Ouch!

In one global corporation, the transition to matrix management meant that the employees at the installation in India would now be reporting to functional supervisors in California. There was still a role for the Managing Director of the facility in India but that role was going to change, with hiring and firing occurring from the California headquarters. Does this mean that California would make these decisions without consultation with key staff in India? No, certainly not. On the other hand, the somewhat parochial or paternalistic arrangement that had long prevailed at the Bangalore operation would be altered significantly. The Managing Director had personally hired all of the line staff, and had trained and mentored each of the senior staff. Now, he had to let go of many prerogatives that he previously enjoyed so that the matrix organization could thrive. Ouch, again.

It is axiomatic that the introduction of any organizational change meets with resistance. Old habits – and old roles – die hard. People tend to want to continue activities that were successful in the past. Breaking this mold and enforcing new roles and rules is not for the faint of heart. Matrix management presupposes strong committed management.

It also requires rich and rapid communications about issues that matter. Without such communications, the vertical and horizontal lines of the matrix will sag, as will the spirits, talents, and contributions of the people in the matrix.

Visit any organization anywhere and you will be told, "We need to improve communications." This is especially true in the matrix organization, which operates as much on the basis of the power of expertise and information as it does on the power of formal positional authority. A core component of meaningful communications is a shared view of the advantages of matrix management. If these are not understood and embraced by everyone who will be learning the new way of doing business, then why bother?

Is Matrix Management Right for Your Organization?

Matrix management is not right for every organization. About a decade ago, the new CFO of an 18,000-employee federal agency asked me to assess the appropriateness of matrix management for her organization. I donned my scuba gear and dove into a series of individual and group interviews with her key people. My recommendation was that she not pursue matrix management. Why? The reason for my recommendation was simple: The politics that she had inherited in her new organization were just plain toxic. The possibilities for sharing objectives, let alone resources, were slim to none. Longstanding traditions of infighting and executive freelancing augured matrixing failure.

There is no point in organizing for cross-functional collaboration if the potential benefits of such synergy are meager. For most organizations, the move to matrix management will stimulate cultural change.

Cultural change emerges from individual changes in behavior. Individual changes in behavior will prompt changes in that employee's attitudes and opinions, not *vice versa*. Changes in behavior lead to changes in attitude and these, in turn, lead to cultural changes.

But what is your organization's degree of readiness for the shift to matrix management? The **Matrix Readiness Abbreviated Self-Appraisal** provides a tool for assessing how your enterprise might adjust to matrix management. I emphasize, however, that the self-appraisal is abbreviated and should not discourage those who are prepared to make the necessary leadership commitments required to change.

A Concluding Thought

Improvements in speed and agility, cross-functional collaboration, goal focus, and other benefits can be achieved through matrix management. However, effective matrix organizations make the necessary investments in ensuring that a common vocabulary is shared to describe the matrixed approach and to ensure that clear roles are established and played effectively without backsliding to longstanding hierarchical traditions. This means change from top to bottom – from a leader who must abandon Darwinian Management to everyone else who must now become a boundary spanner with a 360º mental map of the matrixed organizational structure.

Matrix Readiness Abbreviated Self-Appraisal

Motivational Sufficiency	5-Strongly Agree 4-Agree 3-Don't Know 2-Disagree 1-Strongly Disagree	1	2	3	4	5
1. Customer focus is a priority of increasing importance.						
2. Expansion and integration of product/ service lines to increase convenience and value for the customer is viewed as critical to future success.						
3. The problems that the organization must solve are increasingly complex and multi-functional.						
4. Increasing organizational speed and agility, i.e., reducing the amount of time it takes to get things done is seen as critical.						
5. Organizational learning and creativity are highly valued.						
6. A real or impending crisis caused by competitor actions, technology changes, or other environmental shifts is perceived widely.						
7. Current organizational structure is seen as being out of breath and out of tune with recent changes in strategy and/or systems.						
Top Leadership Patience and Perseverance	5-Strongly Agree 4-Agree 3-Don't Know 2-Disagree 1-Strongly Disagree	1	2	3	4	5
8. Leadership typically requires that all major initiatives are supported by a thought-out implementation plan prior to giving the "green light".						
9. Leadership is willing to deploy training, group facilitation, and coaching resources to usher change as needed and is prepared to require participation by key players regardless of the pressing day-to-day business.						

Matrix Readiness Abbreviated Self-Appraisal *(cont'd)*

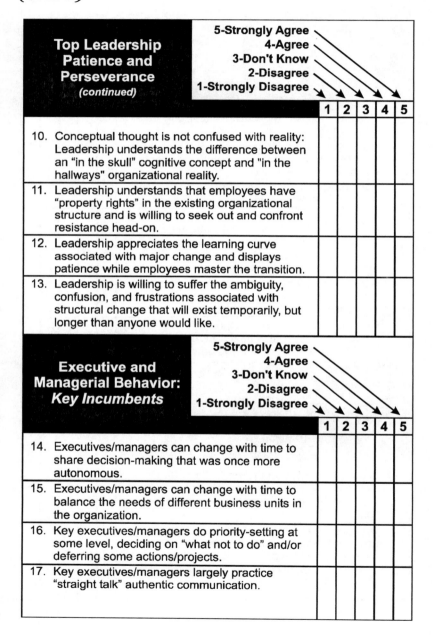

Top Leadership Patience and Perseverance *(continued)*	5-Strongly Agree 4-Agree 3-Don't Know 2-Disagree 1-Strongly Disagree				
	1	2	3	4	5
10. Conceptual thought is not confused with reality: Leadership understands the difference between an "in the skull" cognitive concept and "in the hallways" organizational reality.					
11. Leadership understands that employees have "property rights" in the existing organizational structure and is willing to seek out and confront resistance head-on.					
12. Leadership appreciates the learning curve associated with major change and displays patience while employees master the transition.					
13. Leadership is willing to suffer the ambiguity, confusion, and frustrations associated with structural change that will exist temporarily, but longer than anyone would like.					
Executive and Managerial Behavior: *Key Incumbents*	5-Strongly Agree 4-Agree 3-Don't Know 2-Disagree 1-Strongly Disagree				
	1	2	3	4	5
14. Executives/managers can change with time to share decision-making that was once more autonomous.					
15. Executives/managers can change with time to balance the needs of different business units in the organization.					
16. Key executives/managers do priority-setting at some level, deciding on "what not to do" and/or deferring some actions/projects.					
17. Key executives/managers largely practice "straight talk" authentic communication.					

Matrix Readiness Abbreviated Self-Appraisal *(cont'd)*

Executive and Managerial Behavior: *Key Incumbents* (continued)	5-Strongly Agree / 4-Agree / 3-Don't Know / 2-Disagree / 1-Strongly Disagree	1	2	3	4	5
18. By and large, key executives/managers do not "shoot the messenger," particularly if the messenger brings potential solutions.						
19. To some extent, key executives/managers have migrated away from traditional "command-and-control" behaviors.						
20. The overstatement of requirements or deadlines, bluster, and threats are tactics that are seldom seen and besides, they don't work well in this culture.						
21. Relationship skills and emotional intelligence are viewed as important by key executives/managers.						
22. Key executives/managers seek information, input and clearance from various functional areas prior to making major, complex decisions.						
23. There is an healthy, eclectic appetite for new knowledge, skills and approaches that avoids "flavor-of-the-month" management fads and fashions.						
Organizational Context, Culture & History	5-Strongly Agree / 4-Agree / 3-Don't Know / 2-Disagree / 1-Strongly Disagree	1	2	3	4	5
24. Roles and responsibilities in the current organizational structure are clearly defined.						
25. Key Result Areas/Critical Success Factors are clearly communicated.						
26. Accountable performance metrics are reviewed regularly and action implications are sorted out.						

Matrix Readiness Abbreviated Self-Appraisal *(cont'd)*

Organizational Context, Culture & History *(continued)*	5-Strongly Agree 4-Agree 3-Don't Know 2-Disagree 1-Strongly Disagree	1	2	3	4	5
27. Resource constraints are identified explicitly and are managed realistically.						
28. Staff are willing to take some risks rather than always just waiting for detailed "from-above" guidance and direction.						
29. Various organizational components believe that their fate is shared with other components; the thought of pursuing shared objectives using shared resources would not cause an outburst of uncontrollable laughter.						
30. Staff have <u>not</u> been bombarded with a series of recent organizational changes that didn't "take" or otherwise failed to achieve full and credible implementation.						

Scoring Key

To assess your organization's readiness or appropriateness for adopting a matrix organization and management structure, please use your answers to the Self-Appraisal Questionnaire to fill in the blanks below.

Motivational Sufficiency   **Score**
Total of numbers circled for Items 1-7:   _____ ÷ 7 = _____

Top Leadership Patience & Perseverance   **Score**
Total of numbers circled for Items 8-13:   _____ ÷ 6 = _____

Executive & Managerial Behavior: *Key Incumbents*   **Score**
Total of numbers circled for Items 14-23:   _____ ÷ 10 = _____

Organizational Context, Culture & History   **Score**
Total of numbers circled for Items 24-30:   _____ ÷ 7 = _____

Now, examine your organization's scores for these four categories. Scores of 3.5 or less in any category indicates that your organization may want to plan and implement some interim change initiatives prior to adopting the matrix form of organization.

Discussion of Scoring Key

This Abbreviated Self-Appraisal is just that, *abbreviated* and should be used with caution. A series of high scores in all four categories should not be interpreted as a sufficient condition for moving forward with matrix management. Similarly, a series or low scores should not daunt the organization that believes that the matrix structure is its best option to organize people in a way that is aligned with its chosen strategies and systems.

The Self-Appraisal is based on observations drawn over several years from organizations found in a wide variety of industries that have pursued the matrix structure. It is based on the demonstrated fact that current behavior is predictive of future behavior to a significant degree. While changes in individual and organizational behavior can and do occur, the scope and magnitude of these changes tend to be incremental. If some of the behavioral ingredients of the successful matrix organization are already available in whole or in part, the probability of successful matrix implementation rises accordingly.

The reasoning behind each of the categories is explained briefly in the following paragraphs.

Motivational Sufficiency

Organizations change strategies and systems with some regularity. However, changes to structure tend to be avoided. Changes in organizational structure are viewed as the equivalent of touching a highly electrified "third rail" because employees have "property rights" in the existing structure and, at the risk of understatement, prefer the known to the unknown. For this reason, there really needs to be a *bona fide* urgency that is sufficient to motivate the leadership and staff of the enterprise to embrace structural change. Structural change is not only inconvenient, it is often painful to individuals and, for a brief period, to organizational productivity. If motivation is inadequate unto the day, the tedious work of changing roles, relationships among roles, and other structural shifts is work unlikely to be completed. Matrix management failures are as often attributable to motivational problems as they are to organizational capability.

Top Leadership Patience and Perseverance

It is right that cerebral people run today's organizations. The danger is that leaders too often confuse executive thinking with organizational reality. Sometimes the two are the same and sometimes they are not. When there is variance between the organizational concept held on "mahogany row" and the reality that exists in the hallways and field offices, frustrations will emerge that tax the patience and perseverance that are essential to successful implementation of a new organizational form. Leaders must be ready, willing, and able to guide the enterprise through the foggy seas of transitioning from one organizational form that has been relatively certain during the past to one that is more uncertain for the future. The "drive-by organization" consisting of a memo or two, a brief all-hands meeting, accompanied by a revised organizational chart is not sufficient for accelerated and successful implementation of the matrix structure. Conversion to the matrix structure need not take forever and it need not consume undue resources, but mere willfulness, hope and magic won't get the job done.

Executive and Managerial Behavior: *Key Incumbents*

Executive and managerial behavior must have already evolved to a modern level that is collaborative, emotionally intelligent, savvy in navigating internal politics, and typified by authentic communications. If executive and managerial behavior has fossilized into "silo" and/or "command-and-control" patterns, the odds for behavioral flexibility and change required by the matrix structure are likely to be unfavorable, although not necessarily impossible.

Organizational Context, Culture, and History

A herd of timid staff awaiting detailed guidance and pursuing unclear objectives is going to find the transition to a matrix organization to be difficult at best. In addition, an organization that has a tradition of clearly defining roles and responsibilities is likely to continue its good organizational hygiene in a matrix organization where such clarity is even more essential than in a traditional vertical hierarchy. In addition, an organization with a history of toxic politics where organizational components do not cooperate with each other very well is going to find the cultural changes associated with the matrix organization to be formidable indeed.

CHAPTER 2:

One Size Matrix Does Not Fit All:
Designing Your Matrix

In a meeting recently with the CEO of a major company in Detroit, I became aware of yet another implication of the term "matrix management."

"I am not looking to matrix the entire organization from stem to stern," the CEO said adamantly. He was concerned that my use, or for that matter, anyone's use of the term "matrix management" conveyed the connotation that every nook and cranny of the enterprise would be "turned upside down." He mistakenly assumed that if you have seen one matrix organization you have seen them all. When it comes to matrix management, one size certainly does not fit all.

Following this conversation, it occurred to me that I should address the idea of customizing matrix management to suit a range of needs and preferences. I have discussed these possibilities in greater depth in my Matrix Immersion Training, but this book communicates the fundamentals more widely in the hope that more people will appreciate the flexibility of matrix management.

First of all, it is a matter of conscious executive choice as to which functions shall be matrixed and which shall not. The design decision here refers to defining what is "inside the matrix" and what is "outside the matrix." Stated differently, it is your choice as to which functions come to be represented on your horizontal matrix teams.

For example, in working with a global pharmaceutical company based in Switzerland, headquarters made it plain to U.S. operations: Thou shall not matrix the finance function. Finance will be handled directly by headquarters and it will not be matrixed there or anywhere else – period. Apart from the Swiss conviction that no one can manage money better than they – and they may well be right – this choice indicated the CEO's insistence on controlling directly and closely both the horizontal and vertical issues and decisions related to finance. In other words, the top global leadership team will make both strategic and tactical decisions about all financial issues!

Beyond deciding which functions are either "inside" or "outside" the matrix, however, the overarching executive decision is to define the real purpose and scope of the matrix organization. What benefits do you seek from cross-cutting collaboration? What unique synergies should be facilitated and released? What interfaces should be highlighted and bolstered? Are these cross-cutting benefits, synergies, and interfaces strategic or tactical in nature or are they both?

The continuum, shown below, displays the range of options – from the strategic to the tactical – to discern the purpose and scope of matrix management for your enterprise:

Continuum of Matrix Management Design Options: Strategic to Tactical

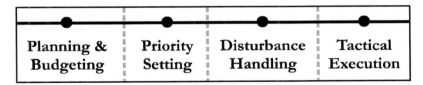

| Planning & Budgeting | Priority Setting | Disturbance Handling | Tactical Execution |

Each anchor on this continuum represents a point at which you can start or stop the design of a matrix organization to fit your needs. Nothing in this continuum should be construed to mean that you start on the left side and "evolve" inevitably to the right, i.e., tactical, side. There is no need to "graduate" to the next level because there is no "next" level, only the matrix management focus that is just right for *your* organization.

Each of the four major points along the continuum is explained below.

Planning and Budgeting. For instance, an enterprise that is interested in promoting a one-organization concept centered on carefully defined cross-cutting goals may prefer the *Planning and Budgeting* model where cross-disciplinary teams are formed and deployed for purposes of strategic and annual planning, and budgeting. The intention here is to ensure that each function's objectives, activities, and budgets have been aligned and harmonized with your organization's core goals, concentrating the use of resources to achieve synergistic benefits and minimizing the amount of function-centric "freelancing" that adds little or no value to the enterprise.

The use of plans and budgets ensures that all resource-consuming activities can be tied to core goals. They are particularly important in scientific and technical organizations where the tendency to freelance becomes very difficult to police. For example, one can understand the desire of drug-development scientists to prepare and present papers at scientific forums and conferences. While these events provide an opportunity to share information, recruit talent, and build the company's reputation, the simple truth is that pharmaceutical companies are not academic institutions. This professional activity must be tethered to the company's core product-development goals, and not become a "pet project" of interest to just the scientist.

The matrix interface go-to person for an R&D discipline can render an informed opinion about whether a scientist's research fits the matrix team objectives. If many matrix interface go-to people from the matrix teams conclude that a given body of research does not add value, then R&D management can and should help the scientist shift efforts in a direction more beneficial to the company.

The U.S. National Oceanic and Atmospheric Administration (NOAA) has stood up nearly two dozen goal-focused matrix teams that cut across their separate line offices, e.g., the National Weather Service, National Ocean Service, National Marine Fisheries Service, National Satellite Service, and more. These teams are responsible for the attainment of specific goals contained in the NOAA strategic plan. These goals are multi-disciplinary and promote integrated science, product/service, public policy, and action relative to such topics as coral reef preservation, control of invasive fish species, coastal management, and transportation weather (air, land, and sea). The charter of each matrix goal team is to ensure that the goals, objectives, and budgets developed by each of the specialty vertical line offices further the cross-cutting goals of the matrix team so that each issue area – for instance, preserving coral reefs – is fully integrated.

When planning and budgeting is conducted in an exacting manner, overseen by executives who ensure that maximum value is being added in way that is consistent with the strategic plan of the organization, matrix management is a powerful way to ensure that there is cross-functional integration and a one-organization concept, and that "freelancing" is kept to a minimum.

Priority Setting. Priority setting goes beyond higher-order planning and budgeting described above. Priority setting is a bit more invasive into operations – it functions at a lower altitude and focuses on a closer level of detail. It is the matrix governance overlay that is used to ensure that priorities set throughout the organization are harmonious and complementary rather than contradictory. As with all design choices, this matrix organization option has implications for cross-functional team charters and for the resultant roles and responsibilities that will be set forth for leaders and key individuals.

For instance, take a business that manufactures a specialized appliance for both commercial and residential purposes. As you might predict, there are significant commonalities associated with the commercial and residential application of this product. However, there are some important differences as well, and these differences have significant implications for manufacturing production. In this business, the eternal tension between production and sales gets as hot as a stove-top burner. Manufacturers of the product must accommodate the competing priorities of each market segment and its respective sales force. Matrix teams bring together representatives from the marketing and sales, finance, engineering, and manufacturing operations to prevent dueling priorities and to smooth production schedules in a cost-sensible and customer-focused way.

Disturbance Handling. Going further, it may make sense for some enterprises to extend beyond *Planning and Budgeting* and *Priority Setting* and focus the power of matrix management on *Disturbance Handling* to avert train wrecks and resolve frequent dueling priorities that cannot be handled during the customary planning/budgeting/priority-setting cycles. In this model, the matrixed teams apply criteria that define problems that are big and weighty enough to warrant cross-disciplinary attention and action. One typical benefit sought by this matrix design is correction of the "one-hand-doesn't-know-what-the-other-hand-is-doing" syndrome. The horizontal matrix team is responsible for ensuring internal integration, coordination, and for resolving – and preventing – dueling priorities.

R&D efforts at pharmaceutical companies are often matrix-managed from this vantage point. When one compound doesn't seem to hold much promise, or otherwise loses attractiveness against another compound that seems like a better investment, there is a "disturbance." The disturbance occurs because a number of bench scientists located at various laboratories across the globe are going to need to shift their focus from one compound to another. There will be other shifts related to finance and infrastructure. The matrix team manages such disturbances on a cross-functional basis usually organized by product, e.g., cardiovascular drugs, neuro-psychiatric drugs, oncological drugs, etc.

One client, the nation's 12th largest school system, used matrix teams organized by geography for disturbance-handling purposes. After an elementary school burned to the ground one night, the matrix team responsible for that neighborhood mobilized. The go-to person for facilities swung into action and accessed the resources of the entire school district, coordinating with his counter-parts systemwide. Other team members coordinated with their counterparts to find temporary services for the displaced students. While an event of this significance certainly had the attention of the system's top leadership, decisions and work didn't bottleneck at the top. Thanks to the matrix, the disturbance was successfully managed at every level.

Tactical Execution. Finally, some organizations want matrix management expressed fully and in its entirety, extending all the way from strategic and operational planning and budgeting, through day-to-day operations. For these organizations – typically those involved in complex product development or service delivery – the penetration of the matrix goes well beyond the "govern-ance overlay" and lives deep within middle management layers.

The first matrix organizations 50 years ago in the aircraft-manufacturing business operated at the tactical execution level because the matrix organization needed to manage multiple projects using a shared pool of resources. Similar matrix organizations subsequently arose in such indus-tries as information technology and pharmaceutical R&D.

In point of fact, this final *Tactical Execution* anchor on the continuum was the mental image that was making our Midwestern CEO uncomfortable about matrix management and its implications. The "tactical execution" model was the one that he did not want. The model he prefers stops and starts at governance, particularly planning and budgeting. The good news for him and for everyone else is that choices about how deeply a matrix organization should penetrate your operations are available. Indeed, it is a conscious choice that *must* be made and talked about explicitly. There is no one-size-fits-all matrix.

A Concluding Thought

While there are some fundamental rules that need to be observed if matrix management success is to be achieved, there is considerable flexibility in customizing the design of your matrix organization to suit your needs. By exercising design freedom, you can tailor a matrix organization that works for you. It is important to communicate your design and its underlying rationale to employees. This is especially critical for employees who may have worked in a different type of matrix organization elsewhere earlier in their careers – employees, like our Midwestern CEO – who need to be disabused of the idea that if you have seen one matrix you have seen them all.

CHAPTER 3:

Matrix Success Leadership Factors

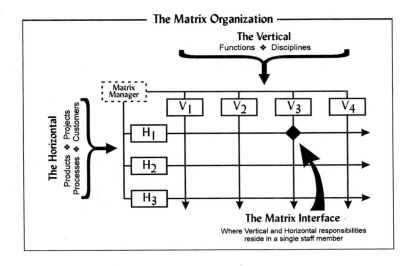

What Does it Take to Be a Matrix Virtuoso?

If you are like most executives who are leading any sort of reorganization, you may be concerned about managers and staff spending too much time focusing inward on organizational process issues. You are right to be concerned about process issues lingering for too long as front-burner priorities, whether in the move to matrix management or to some other organizational structure. On the other hand, there is considerable danger that your reorganization will not "take" if you turn attention away prematurely from role clarification, the definition of vertical team responsibilities and prerogatives, horizontal team responsibilities and prerogatives, and work process accountability.

The temptation to declare victory prematurely – to say that the reorganization is now firmly in place and fully operational – is profoundly powerful. However, yielding to this temptation can do considerable damage. The danger is that employees will not understand what they are expected to do differently as a result of the restructuring and will wait for the reorganization to collapse of its own weight. Rather than declaring "time's up!" on internal role and process negotiations before new pathways have been forged, you may want to clarify your timetable for when key players should reach agreement on the major role and process issues in your matrix organization, making it plain when you expect them to accept organizational imperfection and focus on the productive business.

One client executive became concerned that the many meetings about the matrix reorganization would never end and wanted to issue a cease-and-desist order to get his organization back to the business at hand. I advised him to solicit from the key players a description of remaining implementation efforts and their proposed timetable for completing these tasks, with an eye to negotiating a faster timetable. This approach avoided leaving "issues hanging," expedited the process, and extinguished any tendencies to engage in navel-gazing.

You don't want to micromanage every role and work process, however. Doing so robs the matrix of the very flexibility and freedom that it is designed to bring. On the other hand, the hard work needed to get the matrix structure into place – defining the tasks, negotiating the timetable, and educating the key players – simply cannot be avoided. We all need to walk before we run.

No, we don't want to encourage managers and staff to be infatuated with process. Our purpose is to ensure that there is just enough clarity to function with a minimum of confusion and consternation. The staff should recognize that the matrix is merely the "scaffolding" for shoring up the more important organizational ends. Like all scaffolding, it will eventually be discarded because the lasting structure, created through honest toil, will be freestanding.

The Matrix Success Leadership Model

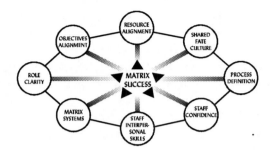

As discussed previously, each organization that opts for matrix management does so for its own special set of reasons that usually relate to speed, creativity, organizational learning, increased customer focus, and improved ability to manage complexity toward attainment of cross-cutting goals.

Achieving the benefits of matrix management does not happen by wishing, by hoping, or by chance. *The Matrix Success Leadership Model* can help you obtain the advantages of matrix management.

Resource Alignment

It is important to align your resources because the matrix is quite unforgiving of mismatches between needs, priorities, and available resources. In the matrix, such mismatches cannot be finessed incessantly at the top management level between captains of two organizational stovepipes. Instead, in a thriving matrix, the mismatches are "lived" at the staff matrix interface level where the vertical and horizontal axes of the organization meet. This means that tough political decisions about resources are best made at the top of the organization and at the front end of organizational process, so that the entire enterprise isn't overwhelmed by disruptive staff disputes that may arise from resource decisions. When managers, let alone staff, are confronted with politics for which they have insufficient power and/or savvy to deal with, the results are gridlock, cynicism, masquerade, postponement, and, most importantly, stalled momentum.

One client had a major account with Wal-Mart along with other smaller accounts from companies such as K-Mart, Target, Dollar General, and others. Wal-Mart is, of course, the two-ton gorilla in the retail marketplace with a reputation for throwing its weight around with vendors. The client had organized its matrix teams by customer. The natural tilt of the organization was toward the Wal-Mart team. The question of the day was always, "What does Wal-Mart want?"

Extraordinary effort was required to ensure that all clients, in addition to Wal-Mart, received the high-quality service for which the client company was known. Explicit and courageous decision making was needed at the top to ensure that Wal-Mart did not capsize services to the other customers. Leaving these decisions to lower-echelon staff to "work out" would have been an irresponsible approach by top management.

In my travels, I often hear people say that matrix management *introduces* "too much politics" into the organization. I respond to this by saying that there are always politics in any organization that does not possess unlimited resources – and few organizations have endless assets. I also point out that resource-driven politics can overwhelm any organization – including a matrix organization – if the necessary "heavy lifting" decision making does not occur at the top.

Here are some suggestions to consider for precise resource planning and management:

- ❑ Take a clear-eyed look at active projects and processes and the resources they require. Measure human resources in person-hours. In addition, don't neglect facilities, information technology, and other means of production that will be useful. Force participants in your matrix organization to stretch resources, but don't allocate a mere teacup of fuel for a cross-country journey.

- ❑ Implement an organized forum of designated decision-makers who examine competing priorities, hear businesses cases, and match resource demand with resource supply in a way that is viewed as fair and reasonable even though no one gets everything he or she wants.

I worked with a company that had developed a formula for resource priority setting that was driven by the company's strategic plan. The formula contained several variables that had been weighted in accordance with the strategic plan's core goals. When a funding request for a major program or project was introduced, "rating points" were attached to the proposal using the variables derived from the strategic plan. This resulted in a point-scored rank-ordering of projects against the pot of available money. Anything above the "available resources" line was funded, and anything "below the line" was excised or deferred accordingly.

Objectives Alignment

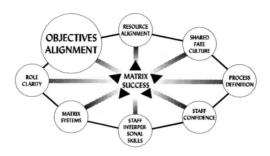

Just as the matrix is unforgiving of chronic resource insufficiency, it is also unforgiving of incompatible objectives. If the vertical leadership of a discipline is advocating a particular approach across and within each horizontal team and the horizontal leadership is pursuing objectives that are incompatible with that approach, life at the matrix interface will be somewhere between misery and ineffectiveness.

If the horizontal team is seeking to provide value to customers based on state-of-the-art innovation, while one or more vertical teams are investing inadequately in innovation, we have an example of misaligned objectives.

Take a close look at the objectives of each vertical and horizontal component in the matrix to identify and resolve inconsistencies and conflicts. Make sure that each matrix interface staff member is meeting one-on-one with his or her vertical leader and horizontal leader so they can identify and resolve differences in direction or emphasis.

If your organization has a fairly sophisticated planning process already in place, the identification of conflicting goals and objectives is something that you have already mastered. Other organizations may need to develop review processes and responsibilities that will surface and "interrogate" them until there is harmony among all goals and objectives.

A public-sector example might shed light on what I am saying. Assume we have a goal-focused horizontal matrix team whose purpose is to ensure that invasive fish species are minimized and eliminated in U.S. waters. One of the team's vertical functions is responsible for the fleet of research vessels that do tests and experiments related to oceanography, ocean weather, marine biology, and more. Part of the "interrogation" will be to ensure that the amount of "research time" on the ships in the fleet is adequate for the containment of invasive fish, but balanced with the myriad competing research objectives that also want ship time.

Role Clarity

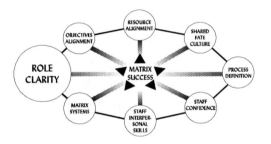

The importance of role clarity cannot be overstated. Conceptualizing the matrix organization is easier than implementing it. Too many executives assume that managers and staff will magically know what to do as the matrix management approach is adopted. Too many executives use a "drive-by reorganization"™ approach to lay out a diagram, a few concepts, and answer a few employee questions. You can't "will" the matrix into place. It takes new understandings and deliberate efforts.

What am I supposed to do differently? That's the question that the employees want answered whenever there is an organizational change. You can safely predict that most employees will find matrix management a bit bewildering at first. They need help understanding what it is, how it works, and what's in it for them.

We introduced the Basic Matrix Role Dichotomy or "role splitter" concept in Chapter 1, but we repeat here once again because it is so central to the successful operation of the matrix organization.

Matrix Role Splitter

Horizontal Team Leader	Vertical Functional Leader
❖ What is to be done?	❖ How will the task be done?
❖ When will the task be done?	❖ Where will the task be done?
❖ Why will the task be done?	❖ Who will do the task?
❖ How much money is available to do the task?	❖ How well has the functional input been integrated into Horizontal Unit efforts?
❖ How well has the total effort been done?	

Several years ago, I performed work for a pharmaceutical company in New Jersey, which was seeking to improve the functioning of its matrix organization. Upon interviewing some of the key players I kept running up against the notion of "shared responsibility." The vertical and horizontal leadership responsibilities had been blurred to the extent that a great deal of confusion, conflict, and cynicism were the inevitable results. In fact, this notion of "shared responsibility" had created full employment for a major consulting firm that had literally pulled a large trailer onto the company campus and was running consultants in and out of meetings for conflict resolution. The chronic blurring of responsibilities made for never-ending conflicts and a wealth of billable hours for a consulting operation that I can only call parasitic. The introduction of the *Basic Matrix Role Dichotomy* was sufficiently helpful that my client was able to invite the consulting firm to remove its trailer and get on down the road.

Matrix Systems

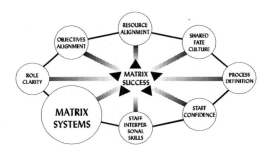

Systems that support matrix management require adaptation of existing systems and, in some cases, development of new systems. Several supporting systems are addressed in the discussion below, namely:

- ❏ Human Resource Systems
- ❏ Budgeting and Financial Tracking Systems
- ❏ Production and Project Tracking Systems

Human Resource Systems. The matrix organization requires adjustments to human resource systems. For example, the vertical organization is the "home base" for the employee, deploying each staff member as it sees fit. In this way, a matrix assignment is not a "dedicated personnel assignment." Ideally, a given staff member playing the matrix interface role should be moved around the matrix to keep both teams and individuals fresh. What's more, staff growth and development is aided by such periodic rotation.

Additional matrix assignments help staff members understand that a matrix assignment is an integrated blend of the horizontal and vertical – akin to carrying two portfolios – rather than as an arrangement where the employee spends X percent of her time working for Boss 1 and X percent of her time working for Boss 2. Whenever I interview staff and they describe matrix management as an arrangement where they "split their time" between two bosses, I know that this is a matrix that is not achieving its potential and may be causing problems. A common complaint levied against matrix management is that it's used to get the work of two employees out of just one staff member by having two bosses double-team him. Rather than the "split time" model, we need an integrated blend where the matrix interface staff member – the "go-to" person – is bringing her home function's agenda to the team and her matrix team's agenda to her home function.

For example, let's assume a matrix team that is responsible for sales of over-the-counter pharmacy products to the giant chain of CVS Pharmacies. The horizontal matrix team is organized by customer, i.e., CVS. The team consists of representatives for oral health care products, feminine health care products, smoking cessation products, and more. The matrix team is responsible for integrated selling to CVS with the objectives of maximizing market and wallet share. The go-to team member for oral hygiene products brings the oral hygiene product objectives to the CVS team, but also brings the CVS team's objectives home to oral hygiene. It's a two-way street consisting of both/and perspectives and negotiation, rather than either/or.

❑ Vertical and horizontal input in each staff member's personnel evaluation must be the rule not the exception, as long as each participating manager has a standing to evaluate. This means that the horizontal leader used the staff member's services at a significant level to justify participating in the personnel's appraisal.

❑ There's never a good time for education and training, and in the matrix, the complexity of scheduling learning opportunities becomes *at least* twice as difficult. Individual Development Plans and iron-fisted human resource authority that ensures that learning occurs within broadly specified timeframes is essential so that matrixed staff are not neglected when it comes to training and development.

One example from a few years ago comes to mind. In a company that develops and sells electrical power, the IT staff had been matrixed across the operating divisions in an effort to get close to their internal customers. When I conducted focus groups with the IT employees regarding their concerns about matrix management, the most frequent lament was that it had become more difficult for these professionals to stay abreast of new developments in the IT field and that going to training had become "twice as hard," because now they needed both vertical and horizontal approvals to get training. First of all, the vertical leader for IT is responsible for the quality of personnel who serve the operating divisions – both now and in the future. As stated previously, there is never a good time for training, and IT's internal customers will resist any potential disruption of service because staff is absent. However, training is integral to the ability of the workforce to deliver quality services both today and tomorrow. The vertical leader is responsible for getting these staff to training *and* quelling any outbreaks of customer dissatisfaction. No one promised that the job of the vertical leader was going to be easy even though the **Basic Matrix Role Dichotomy** has dispatched some traditional responsibilities to the horizontal leaders.

· **Budgeting and Financial Tracking Systems.** I have never encountered a major matrix management implementation that didn't require changes in budgeting and financial tracking systems. Period. Traditional budgeting and financial tracking systems mirror traditional hierarchical organizations, meaning there is a budget for marketing and sales, for engineering, for manufacturing, for R&D, etc.

In a matrix we want to know budgets and expenses by function, but also by function within the horizontal team, and by the horizontal team as a whole. We want to foot and cross-foot, reflecting both the vertical life and the horizontal life of the organization. We want to review budgets and expenses both vertically and horizontally. This inevitably requires changes to legacy systems, which typically budget and track vertically, but not horizontally.

Again, it should be no surprise that a move to integrated selling of over-the-counter health products will involve changes in budgeting and financial tracking systems so that we no longer just have stand-alone budgeting and tracking for, say, toothpaste, feminine napkins, and anti-smoking patches, but we have integrated selling budgets and tracking for CVS, Rite-Aid, Wal-Mart, Safeway, and other retail outlets that are the targets of business-to-business selling.

Production and Project Tracking Systems. One global corporation was particularly concerned with ensuring that their "balanced scorecard" dashboards were compatible with their new matrix organization.

Matrix management is intended to weaken functional compartmentalization. Matrix teams are in business to solve problems collaboratively and to be accountable for collective outcomes. Matrix team members each bring a somewhat different viewpoint and understanding of customer requirements. The challenge is to bridge these understandings so that measurements of the value chain from beginning to end reflect such collaboration. Major balanced scorecard categories, e.g., customer, financial, learning and growth, etc. need to be explored in the context of opportunities and changes caused by adoption of matrix management. Just as with budgeting and financial tracking, the balanced scorecard measures should reflect the vertical and horizontal dimensions of the enterprise.

In a classic matrix organization, structured by horizontal matrix teams that are calling on a shared pool of project personnel, the challenges to person-hour planning and tracking by specialty discipline are considerable. Many a project-centered matrix organization has collapsed of its own weight because internecine squabbles over scarce staff talent overtook the organization's ability to get work done. The antidote to this unhappy situation is to first ensure that there is a complete inventory of staff skills. Second, know how many person-hours are available by specialty. Third, know how many person-hours of a particular specialty have been committed and how many remain available for deployment. I have seen this done quite methodically for IT specialists, showing their hours of commitment to multiple projects and displaying the balance available. Software by Zorch (www.zorchsoftware.com) is one matrix-savvy resource allocation and usage tool that displays staff availability in real time.

Staff Interpersonal Skills

In a traditional hierarchy, a staff member can communicate "up and over" to another functional department through his or her manager. Traditional management theory calls this "up and over" approach the "scalar principle," meaning that the message must scale up to an echelon that has been authorized to communicate with his or her counterpart in some other department.

The scalar principle is just plain slow. The speed of business today requires rapid communication across functions – without delay. Cross-functional teams are a way of bypassing the scalar principle, particularly when the representative from a given function understands that she or he is responsible for keeping functional management fully briefed.

With that said, there is an unspoken assumption for purposes of cross-functional communication and collaboration. The assumption is that team members will have the requisite skills to see beyond their own function and to communicate effectively with people from other functions. It's a higher level of expectation when it comes to interpersonal skills. Why? In a matrix, staff draw less on the formal "power of the boss," and more on their own personal powers of communication, persuasion, negotiation, and problem solving. In a matrix, we assume that the staff interface person has the interpersonal skills needed to smooth ruffled feathers and to communicate and collaborate effectively through the exercise of the power of information and expertise rather than the traditional formal power of position, although that formal power remains available for use in selected instances. In a matrix we no longer assume that the manager routinely picks up the slack when staff evidence deficient interpersonal skills.

In pharmaceutical R&D, drug development is often accomplished by cross-functional matrix teams. For instance, biostatisticians work with regulatory affairs attorneys and registered nurses (RNs) responsible for hospital test protocol implementation as well as with other diverse professionals. Such teams bring together people of differing educations, outlooks, and temperaments. However, their ability to work effectively with one another and to anticipate one another's business concerns can make the critical difference in achieving speed to market in the form of winning Food and Drug Administration (FDA) approval for a new drug. Not surprisingly, statisticians and lawyers don't have a strong natural affinity for one another as a rule! They may need some over-the-shoulder help understanding the potential of their working relationship. That's what I am talking about.

All of this means that some, if not many, matrix interface staff are going to need training and/or coaching in diplomacy and human relations skills to handle dueling priorities, persuasion and negotiation skills, decision-making skills, and techniques for prioritizing and allocating scarce resources in collaboration with other managers and staff.

Training and coaching may be especially necessary for scientific and technical staff who are asked to work cross-functionally. I'll never forget the biotech company bench scientist who told me, in no uncertain terms, that, "If I wanted to work with people, I wouldn't have become a scientist." When we ask employees to leave traditional comfort zones for purposes of implementing new roles and a new organizational concept, we can't just wish the necessary skills into place.

Countless companies have assigned matrix roles without an ounce of training and follow-up support. "Just do it!" may work for Nike, but it doesn't work when we are asking people to do things that they haven't done before or that they really would prefer not to do – given a choice.

Staff Confidence

In a successful matrix, everyone is gaining power even though it may not be immediately apparent. In fact, particularly at the outset of matrix management implementation, I will hear vertical managers complain that they no longer have the status and authority that they enjoyed in the traditional hierarchical organization. Nonetheless, after a time, they concur with me that they have greater influence than they did before. The reason? **Each matrix player has new influence in new realms, both vertical and horizontal.** The vertical manager's leverage in the functional department is greater because the matrix interface staff person is amplifying his or her messages in their respective matrix teams and also with other middle management and frontline functional staff. The vertical manager now has an emissary on the horizontal team who can understand and oblige the preferences of the vertical function.

The matrix structure is a scaffolding for creating a one-firm culture where people talk with one another, curtail end-runs, and focus on resolving the issues. The vertical leader, the horizontal leader, and the staff member at the matrix interface will experience changes. Change is never easy; the leader's job is to help change along as much as possible by building rather than effacing staff confidence.

A personal note may amplify this point. When I took my first job out of college, I had the good fortune to work for several capable managers who were very committed to staff development, mentoring, and coaching. As I look back on those early years in my career, it is now clear that my supervisors sometimes "manufactured" opportunities for me to succeed as a way of building my skills, my reputation, and my confidence. Building staff confidence in the matrix organization suggests the need for a similar "Machiavellian" approach whereby vertical and horizontal leaders "conspire" to help staff achieve success.

Confidence builds as uncertainty diminishes so, to the extent possible, clarify issues such as assignment duration, career visibility, education and training opportunities, personnel evaluations, and career and financial incentives, and encourage staff participation in decision making at all levels.

Communicate matrix successes widely, loudly, and repeatedly. Publicly praise staff members who have taken risks, shown initiative, and who are otherwise demonstrating the expanded technical and interpersonal skills that we hope to cultivate in the matrix.

Process Definition

It helps to clarify relationships among management and staff of the various organizational components so that they don't need negotiation or renewal each day. People are more confident and can step out quickly and smartly if they know the process and their role in it. **Internal Partnership Agreements** should be developed. These need not and should not be lengthy. They should be hammered out in a 60- or 90-minute meeting that is summarized in a page or two. But don't tie things down so tightly that there's no wiggle room or freedom. On the other hand, don't leave things so foggy that you must start from scratch with each new day. Aim at "unstable stability" and you will hit the target. Most organizations find that it helps to cement understandings and expectations about the following concerns:

❑ Standard Operating Procedures

❑ Required lead times

❑ Expected turnaround times and cycle times

❑ Quality specifications

❑ Contacts/protocol

❑ Performance feedback requirements, e.g., type, frequency, means, etc.

❑ Meetings and meeting-management expectations and standards

❑ Issue resolution – who and how

❑ Accountability

The **Lead-Approve-Consult-Inform (LACI) Diagram** is another tool for improving matrix functioning. It is described in depth in Chapter 5. In recent years, many organizations have created process maps in the form of flow-diagrams or other graphic depictions of work activity flow. These process maps should be used to spell out organizational arrangements that will be used in managing the enterprise. Each step in the process is juxtaposed against the roles played in the matrix organization. The responsibility of each role relative to each step is defined in terms of whether the player leads, approves, consults, or merely informs.

The purpose of LACI diagramming is to cut through the bramble bush of "if everyone is responsible, then no one is responsible." I have encountered many organizations where the question "Who approves?" is met with multiple answers such that three or four individuals may be said to "approve" a particular decision. With LACI, this means that the decision has not been reduced to its lowest common denominator, or that roles are particularly unclear, or both. Multiple managers or executives may *consult* on a particular decision, but only one actually *approves*. Much organizational gridlock can be averted with greater clarity about the process, the roles, and who decides, approves, informs, or leads.

Shared Fate Culture

The success of the matrix depends on dynamic, constructive cooperation among the vertical and horizontal components of your organization. Will there still be disputes between vertical leaders and horizontal leaders? Will one horizontal team compete with another horizontal team for scarce resources? You bet! However, such competition needs to occur in the context of a "shared fate" culture where the preferences, let alone the needs, of individual disciplines and organizational components are subordinated to a collective result, which is pursued throughout and across the enterprise.

Don't ignore or deny the entrenched conflicts generated by the natural selfish interests of individuals and their work units. Don't accept thin maskings of these conflicts. Instead, interrogate these conflicts.

I recommend that you bring these conflicts out in the open in a healthy process of competing for resources. In this way, the conflict fuels your strategic agenda rather serving as a time bomb that will ultimately destroy it. Organizational life today is messy in part because constant reinvention and reinvestment is needed if company value is to be maintained, let alone increased. Long-range organizational health and prosperity is really a persistent series of temporary successes. Don't be telegraphic, or, worse, telepathic in communicating shared priorities and expectations. Implement matrix arrangements that are inherently temporary and unstable with the same level of care you would employ in erecting a more permanent structure.

A Concluding Thought

"The perfect is the enemy of the good."

—Voltaire

Do not despair if you don't rate 100 percent on each of these success factors. Most organizations can't, don't, and won't. It's more important that you are improving in each of these areas rather than achieving perfection. We can't wait for every storm to blow over so it's best we learn how to work in the rain. Before moving to the matrix, we were perfectly organized to do the work that we were doing in the way that we were doing it. We may have been perfectly organized to do something well the millionth time, but we were not organized to do another thing the first time.

Increasingly, business is about doing new things and turning on a dime. More often than not, it's a dynamic blend of destruction and innovative experimentation on the one hand, and attempts at perfection of ever-maturing products and services on the other. The speed and agility of matrix management can position us to win in the competitive global marketplace, but implementation requires us to accept the ambiguities of transition along the way.

CHAPTER 4:

Implementing Your Matrix: *If wishes were horses then beggars would ride*

Forces for Change

Three forces are shaking up society: knowledge, education, and entrepreneurialism. Infused in all three is technology – electronics to get the work done with minimal human effort and optimal customer convenience. Add to these forces the rising expectations of customers, shareholders, employees, and others and the result is nothing short of a period of unprecedented change.

Organizations revisit their structural design when they need to rebalance their strategies and systems. Revenue growth pressures, "race-to-the-bottom" cost-reduction initiatives, continuous quality improvements, breakthroughs in responsiveness to customers, and more, are just plain relentless.

Most enterprises do not reorganize constantly. In fact, most organizations avoid it to the maximum extent possible. Indeed, in the March 2006 *Harvard Business Review*, authors Robert S. Kaplan and David P. Norton argue that you can implement new strategies without "disrupting your organization" by adjusting systems to align with strategy and using the balanced scorecard to ensure success. This argument will be accepted enthusiastically by all executives who want to avoid touching the "third rail" of executive life, i.e., designing and implementing changes that alter organizational components, roles and rules of engagement.

It's true that no one should upset the structure needlessly. It *is* disruptive. There will be lost production. There will be a learning curve. There will be resistance and grumbling.

On the other hand, sometimes inexorable pressures call out for structural change. Try as you might, new systems are not always implemented successfully within the existing organizational framework. Sometimes the people, the roles they exercise, and the rules they play by are just plain out of breath. The following situations can hasten the need for structural change:

- *Customers and the Competition* change their behavior, which calls for a significant alteration of the organization's behavior that cannot be attained with mere systems changes.

- *Vendors and Strategic Partners* add or delete capabilities, change approaches radically, increase prices significantly, or effectuate other changes that necessitate modifying the way the organization does business.

- *Top Leadership* arrives and/or departs, prompting structural changes consistent with their assumptions, priorities, experiences, and strategies.

- *Staff* exert pressure for change both overtly and covertly because of increases or decreases in staffing quality and quantity, as well as changing cultural dynamics.

- *Changed Horizontal Processes and Relationships,* in the form of process reengineering and simplification, natural evolution to less hierarchical, more team-based approaches, new adaptations of technology, etc., will blossom only within a new structure.

Whether it's a combination of these factors and/or a mix of the benefits of matrix management that were discussed earlier, a decision to implement matrix management needs to be executed using a step-by-step approach.

Four Major Steps Toward Successful Implementation

There are four major steps that define the pathway to successful implementation:

- ❑ **Step 1**: Analyze the Situation and Identify the Challenges
- ❑ **Step 2**: Plan and Prepare – Communicate!
- ❑ **Step 3**: Lead and Train Your People
- ❑ **Step 4**: Inspect and Correct Dysfunctions

Step 1: Analyze the Situation and Identify the Challenges

Think before you implement. Step 1 is about being aware of your surroundings and thinking about what is going to help you on your way to matrix management success. Let's say that the pressures for structural change have built up to the point where you are ready to make the move to matrix management. You have analyzed the benefits and have concluded that they outweigh the costs. You have considered which matrix management overlay is right for your enterprise – planning and budgeting, disturbance handling, etc. – and have made your choice.

What opportunities for synergy or integration need to be exploited? Which work do teams as opposed to individuals best perform? How will the work be measured so that it can be monitored and controlled?

Take a long, honest look at your current organization. What are the factors that are likely to complicate matrix management success?

Success requires that you identify and neutralize potential obstacles to effective matrix management implementation. Identification of obstacles requires thoughtful analyses of the factors listed below.

- ❑ The logic of the reorganization.
- ❑ The dynamics of today's business climate.
- ❑ The social construction of organizational reality.
- ❑ The organization's history with respect to reorganizations.

Let's take a look at each of these in turn.

The Logic of the Reorganization

Let's reflect on three areas that affect choices about organizational restructuring:

- ❑ Universal Forces
- ❑ Contextual Factors
- ❑ Key Design Drivers

The Universal Forces

Three universal forces may either constrain or enable your plans:

- ❑ Money
- ❑ Stakeholders
- ❑ Technology

Money is a driving force in organizational design decisions. It often is the factor that determines "must do" vs. "nice to do." Money often comes in to play when considering the staffing of the matrix interface positions. More often than not, staff who occupy the positions in the matrix have regular "day jobs" that remain largely unchanged, except that now participation on the matrix team will become yet another duty. Money is going to determine what percentage of the interface staff member's total time will be devoted to matrix team participation. If the organization has more money, it can backfill more of the staff member's other responsibilities and carve out a greater degree of participation in the matrix. This will clearly impact the effectiveness of your matrix organization. If the staff member participates on the matrix team at the "kiss-and-a-promise" level or offers "response-only" involvement, your matrix won't amount to much. The bottom line is this: A worthwhile matrix organization requires a minimal level of investment. You can either afford it or you can't.

I delivered training at the office of one organization that claimed to have implemented matrix management, but, upon my arrival, discovered that they had failed to identify matrix interface members. Their "matrix teams" were strictly theoretical! The teams had never been formed, even though the vertical and horizontal leaders had been designated. They had the sandwich bun, but hadn't spent the money on the meat.

In other instances, I am asked whether it is acceptable to have a key manager serve as both a vertical leader and a horizontal leader under the assumption that the resources aren't there to staff two distinct positions. The correct answer is that it is unacceptable to have a single manager serve as both the vertical and the horizontal leader. Not only does it confuse the manager, it also confuses everyone who must deal with that manager, because it's unclear what role that person is playing at any given moment. It also complicates the role transition for others who are not playing two roles simultaneously.

Part of the power of matrix management is the dynamic tension that exists between the vertical and the horizontal axis. Without the adequate number of players, the organization won't be able to create this lively byproduct of matrix management. It's akin to buying a car, but then not being able to pay for the gas to run it. If you can't afford to staff your matrix properly, hold off until you can.

Stakeholders here refers largely, but not exclusively, to customers. Stakeholders may also refer to stockholders and to board of directors, who can exercise considerable influence over the structure of the enterprise.

In the public sector, and in private for-profit businesses operating in highly regulated industries, the notion of stakeholders extends to Congress (and the legislation it passes), and the federal workers who execute the laws. Legislation defines not only what can be done, but what *must* be done, and often carries with it significant organizational implications for what functions must be kept separated by "Chinese Walls."

The U.S. National Oceanic and Atmospheric Administration (NOAA), for example, didn't need prior congressional approval for its shift to matrix management in 2003, which now permits integrated science to flourish across various line offices, such as the National Weather Service, National Ocean Service, and National Marine Fisheries Service. Congressional approval was not needed because NOAA was not altering its battery of agencies that are overseen by a picket fence of separate Congressional committees. If approval for such an alteration had been sought, the change would have taken untold thousands of person-hours of effort expended over many years. Controversy would be driven by adamant testimony from constituent groups. These groups would be motivated by the implicit and perhaps explicit fear that they would lose their well-defined and familiar points of contact as well as service from the federal government. While their worries likely would have been groundless – matrix management can and will provide superior service and fewer points of contact to get work done – in politics, reality is perception and the wise organization will anticipate both internal and external political concerns.

Under the Criminal Debt Management Act and the Prison Litigation Reform Acts, U.S. Courts are required to coordinate with federal, state, and local prisons. These laws have important implications for organizational design within the federal judiciary. Additional operational, coordination, and reporting processes must be adjusted to comply with the laws – all without the benefit of additional staffing. These may be unfunded add-ons to the existing structure, but they must be dealt with.

Legislation may also stimulate reforms and organizational design changes. The Criminal Justice Reform Act (CJRA), for example, required each of the 94 U.S. District Courts to critically examine their policies and procedures to avoid delays and to save money. Some courts chose to perceive CJRA as a genuine opportunity for positive change and redesigned organizations and procedures accordingly.

Technology and its impact on process redesign and organizational structure could fill up the pages of another entire book. Technology can turn cultures inside out by generating a general resistance to change to complaints that the organization's systems are stuck in the dark ages. Technology often has sweeping impacts on the work that people do, how they do it, and how it gets supervised, both on site and off site. We've only just begun to understand the magnitude of technology-related changes on an organization's structure and functioning.

A global pharmaceutical R&D operation implemented matrix management assisted by all the modern technological conveniences, including interactive videoconferencing. Worldwide virtual matrix teams work on chemical compounds as part of the drug-development effort. The company's worldwide head of information technology explained to scientific staff gathered from throughout the world that technology, combined with matrix management, required fewer physical transfers. Technology-enabled virtual matrix teams bring the work to the worker vs. the other way around.

The Contextual Factors

Organizational design, and implementation decisions and progress, are shaped by their context. Consider this partial list of contextual factors:

- **Chief Officer's Management Style.** Whether it's the CEO or COO, the needs and preferences of the top executive(s) will shape how the enterprise is organized and run. If a new top-level executive arrives on the scene having worked in a successful matrix organization that person is committed to matrix management and its benefits. This dedication makes the critical difference because the executive will not be easily dissuaded.

- **Geographical Dispersal.** While new and exciting virtual teaming is becoming widespread, geography still matters. With a greater emphasis on being closer to the customer, and with Web-enabled participation in organizational life, geography is less important than it was 10 years ago. But face-to-face contact among workers builds trust, loyalty, and understanding, which are impossible to duplicate with technology alone.

- **Human Resource Availability.** Organizing around the strengths and weaknesses of existing personnel is not ideal, but is often reality. An enterprise may possess the necessary financial resources, but lacks adequate talent. If the interpersonal skills of persuasion, negotiation, and boundary-spanning communication are in short supply, the probability of matrix management success may be impossibly low.

- **Facilities Layout and Space Utilization.** The informal organization matters as much or more than the formal organization. The physical space occupied by the organization is where the power of the informal organization often overwhelms the formal organization – frequently with tremendous benefits. For example, if all of the IT people drawn from different units of a public entity are located in the same space, collaboration will often occur spontaneously. I observed an instance where the formal organizational chart, let alone the budget fund codes, neither reflected nor enabled a formal matrix-style sharing of services. However, the physical layout encouraged the IT staff to synergize their work. They shared solutions and equipment, and supported one another's successes. It all happened on the informal level, but for those designing formal structural shifts, it's instructive: The importance of physical proximity in facilities is often underestimated.

Humans' decisions about what is possible in the future tend to be shaped by the past and by their current reality. Take a close look at contextual factors before you finalize your implementation plans.

Key Design Drivers

In his classic 1960's management study, *Strategy and Structure: Chapters in the History of the American Industrial Enterprise*, Alfred D. Chandler, Jr. argued that organizational structure follows strategy. As it turns out, more than four decades later, he was half right. Today's literature reveals that organizational structure does follow strategy *and* that organizational strategy also follows structure.   ·

Chandler was correct that the best organizational thinking seems to begin with strategy as a *conscious* element of organizational design. When organizational thinking begins with "what" and "how," before moving to "who," the thinker will enjoy a broader range of possibilities – literally and figuratively thinking outside of the organizational box.

Fundamentally, high-quality organizational thinking begins with the question: What is most important? By setting clear priorities for designing the organization, more enterprises are making the tough choices between competing attractive alternatives. If a cross-functional approach is critical to achieving goals and serving customers then that probably indicates a matrix design. If functional efficiency makes the business difference and there is limited need for rapid-fire cross-functional synergy, then a more traditional hierarchy may perform superbly.

The following factors are take-off points for implementing organizational change – all of which tend to favor flatter, more collaborative designs. To the extent that these drivers are relevant to your company and industry, they may provide your matrix organizers with a head start or at least a rationale that is already understood by your people as a prevailing trend.

❑ **Efficiency and Economy.** How can the existing infrastructure be maximized? Whether it's the laboratories, the manufacturing equipment, or the fleet, the pressures of cost containment should promote the pursuit of shared objectives using shared resources. Matrix teams working with one another can pinpoint opportunities for resource sharing achieved through compatible scheduling, project piggybacking, and more.

❑ **Customer Satisfaction.** Traditional command-and-control hierarchies are not inherently incompatible with excellent customer service, but a flattened, cross-functional approach to the customer molds the various service facets around the customer rather than the alternative. For example, a CarMax® location's matrix approach to selling and delivering used vehicles employs a team consisting of someone from sales, finance, titling/registration/insurance, and service that envelops the customer. This ensures that the customer is not on a scavenger hunt or worse, is not waiting endlessly while everything needed to complete the transaction is tracked down.

- ❑ **Technological Innovation.** When technological innovation is a high priority and highly visible in your enterprise, it telegraphs the message that future work will not be done as it was in the past. Skill requirements for new and existing staff are defined by high investment in technology, with movement from informal "hobbyist" or self-taught specialists to certified experts who collaborate with experts from other disciplines.

- ❑ **Structural Streamlining.** Streamlining requires the identification of cross-cutting goals and cross-cutting activities that support these goals. Eliminating redundancies and/or activities that do not add value is something that goal-focused matrix teams can do very well. Each matrix interface staff member is in a unique position to identify activities or projects in their function that are not advancing the matrix team's goals and objectives. For instance, let's say that each of seven matrix teams has its own matrix interface staff member representing engineering. Let's say that the engineering interface members meet periodically to compare notes, which, by the way, is something that they should do. In comparing notes, these matrix team members may identify overlapping steps, irrelevancies, or other work efforts that don't add sufficient value. From their unique vantage point in advising vertical management for the engineering function, they are able to identify streamlining opportunities.

- ❑ **Extended Organization/Outsourcing.** It is not always possible – or, for that matter, desirable – to recruit or grow skills that are needed to provide comprehensive solutions. As a result, shared service, outsourcing, or other strategic partnerships may become necessary. LEGO®-toy-style extensions of the "regular" organization through such capability-extending relationships are increasingly common as partnerships snap together and snap apart for various projects of mutual profit and strategic advantage. To the extent that matrix teams are used, the cooperating partner may "connect" as an extended member of the matrix team(s).

The Dynamics of Today's Business Climate

Implementing organizational change requires being mindful of current dynamics and how they will help or hinder the transformation. Our situational analysis presupposes observation, meaning the "reflective power to see." The speed of today's business generates noise or clutter that needs to be factored in to how employees will react to anything, particularly the introduction of unknowns, such as matrix management.

Navigating through the fog that shrouds many organizations these days is important to overcoming implementation obstacles. There are at least three fog banks that need to be pierced:

- ❑ The Chronic Emergency
- ❑ The Grip of the Group
- ❑ Fragile Reality

The Chronic Emergency

A top executive expressed concern about a proposed investment of time and effort needed to organize work relationships and processes. "How can we possibly afford to take people away from what they are doing?" she asked in all sincerity. This sentiment is expressed often because clarifying roles and processes occupies precious time. However, to pierce the fog, managers need to step back two paces and contemplate this riddle: **What work, precisely, will employees be taken away from,**

given that it appears to be relatively unorganized, if not unknown or unmanaged, under the current structure? Are the right people doing the correct jobs in the first place?

If efforts to clarify roles and organize work are thwarted because of perpetual emergencies, one must ask whether this is merely a way of holding on to the current inferior system. Chronic emergency thinking and behavior is a powerful narcotic that lulls people into wanting to keep the status quo.

Businesses do confront genuine emergencies, but if *everything* is an emergency, then you should be more aggressive in separating false emergencies from real ones as a way of understanding your current organization and how it needs to change as matrix management is adopted. Put simply, use the matrix transition as an occasion to redefine what constitutes a *real* emergency and make it clear that you will scrutinize workers who overreact, behaving as if there is a genuine emergency when, in fact, there is not. Above all, do not permit emergencies, real or imaginary, to distract from methodical implementation.

The Grip of the Group

In some organizations, the grip of the group on the individual is iron. By this I mean that employees may suffer from fear of separation from the group, of becoming professionally isolated somehow, or of otherwise being marked as "unable to work effectively with others." If your organization resembles this, it is important that you understand the group dynamics within your organization as you develop your matrix management implementation strategy so that workers aren't inadvertently or accidentally marginalized.

Consider your company's traditions surrounding meetings: attendance is vast, decisions are few, and follow-up is next to nil. In such an organization, employees may complain about wall-to-wall meetings, but may loathe exclusion from any of them because they perceive that the well being of their career relies more on visibility than on genuine contribution. The meeting objectives and agenda also may be undefined or so vague that little good comes of them. Your employees may, in a real sense, be "addicted" to meetings.

The grip of the group may need to be loosened so that you can unfreeze the way things have been to achieve successful implementation. That may include restricting meeting attendance to the vital few.

If you clarify roles, you can help people escape the grip of the group. What kind of meeting is this? Is it information gathering and sharing? Are we building to a decision? Are we making a decision? Who needs to be there and why? Clarifying the objectives of the meeting and the logic of participation in the meeting can go a long way to averting herd-like behavior and allow at least some of the meeting addicts to go "cold turkey!"

Fragile Reality — Transient and Disposable

The speed of modern business can obscure the meaning of certain tasks. Fewer frequent face-to-face contacts can mean that employees have less context or insight as to the "whys" of what they do and how those activities fit together. Making sense of things in the organization gets tougher and reality itself appears to be shifting. Things are this way today and that way tomorrow, often without a lot of explanation. Many of us are accustomed to these "meaning deficits" and have learned to live with them given our lack of time to pause and reflect. However, implementation of structural changes in the organization deserves a bit of reflection on the context and meaning behind the work that is being done.

A pharmaceutical client was going through a period of tumultuous change. Workers were generally dispirited by the seemingly unending waves of change; employees were unclear where the enterprise was headed, unsure of what mattered, and confused about their future roles and contributions. To many of the staff, life was a bit like the old movie, "Brigadoon," where the fog cleared just enough for the magic city to become visible for one day a year. To resolve the confusion, the human resource team recognized that staff of all stripes – from bench scientists to sales executives – needed to discuss what was going on and what it meant. Workers were able to talk to the HR staff, which served as the junction box for generating new understandings that helped get everyone past the turbulent period.

The Social Construction of Organizational Reality

Any valued organization is a pattern of roles and relationships brought to life through shared purpose and united effort. A graphic depiction of the organization – an "organization chart" – offers a limited view at best. A photo of all of the employees standing in an aircraft hanger doesn't show it either.

An organization exists in the many minds of those who participate in it or with it. Stated differently, an organization is a figment of the collective imagination. **It stands to reason that achieving "organization" requires that we maximize the sharing of expectations and perceptions among these many minds.**

Getting the organization implanted in the collective imaginations of people takes some doing. Organizations become embodied in individual experience by means of roles and role-playing. People participate in the workplace through these roles and, as they do, further ratify the existence of the organization. By internalizing these roles, the organization becomes subjectively real to each member of the enterprise. As Peter L. Berger and Thomas Luckmann described in their classic work, *The Social Construction of Reality* (New York: Doubleday Anchor,

1966): "A social world will be in the process of construction, containing within it the roots of an expanding institutional order." Stated differently, human beings implicitly cooperate with one another to define who we are, what we do, and how we relate to one another. As more and more humans connect with one another and spin a reality that is constantly "under construction," we link an expanding number of networks together until the way we perceive things collectively seems to be instinctive to us as individuals. It makes an "organization" seem real to each of us even though no one has ever actually *seen* an "organization" apart from a chart depicting one!

All of this is to emphasize the importance of ensuring that roles are made very clear as part of the implementation process. To achieve this clarification requires that you reflect on your organization's history of defining roles.

Why does this sociology matter? To the extent that undefined or blurred roles are permitted to exist, the social construct – the organizational reality – will be incomplete or defective, usually resulting in employee timidity. Unclear boundaries often stimulate negative fantasies about the risks of overstepping boundaries or tripping over landmines. This stifles creativity and increases "Mother-may-I?" requests for approval prior to taking even the smallest action. Unclear roles and boundaries invite dysfunctional power struggles, and divert energy from mission and goals toward internal processes and relationships – the very things you don't want to dwell on.

To avoid spending too much time on internal processes and relationships, spend some quality time up front on these very topics. To do so effectively requires identifying the extent to which different minds are viewing the past and present a take-off point from radically different perspectives. We'll need to understand this starting point if we are to roll out implementation in a way that gets everyone on board.

I've been the clean-up man on more than a few "ready-fire-aim" or "drive-by" reorganizations. I am happy to do some replanning and implementation support that helps the matrix organization achieve its potential. However, the better way is ready-aim-fire. I have had the pleasure of working with several organizations where executives adopted a careful approach of planning and implementation support prior to "declaring" that the new matrix organization was in full force. Think about which way is better for you and your people and it won't take but an instant for you to reach the right conclusion.

Your Organization's History with Respect to Reorganizations

How recently was your enterprise reorganized? What was the nature and extent of the reorganization? To what degree have frequent and large-scale reorganizations contributed to employee fatigue, cynicism, or slumps in morale? Are we talking about an enterprise that has weathered large organizational changes or smaller fine-tunings? Are we talking about a business that is shell-shocked from wave after wave of major reorganization? Knowing the answers to these questions will help you position implementation favorably and effectively. The history of reorganizations should be assessed as part of your situational analysis. This history may present challenges that must be met head-on.

Reorganizations vary in their frequency and magnitude. A reorganization that is considerable in scope but infrequent, often after a number of years, is a **Big Change.** An organization that makes frequent, small-scale changes is in what I call the **Adjustment** mode. The **Fine-Tuning** approach is characterized by infrequent and minor shifts in structure.

Finally, the **Shell Shocked** characterization applies to an enterprise that has experienced several major reorganizations within the past two or three years. The "here-we-go-again" attitude abounds in this situation. Staffs often assume a "wait-and-see" posture after the reorganization, knowing that another flavor-of-the-month change is around the corner. All of this must factor into matrix planning so that you can plan implementation based on previous lessons learned and sharpen communications about the future in a way that accommodates the past.

Step 2: Plan and Prepare – Communicate!

When an enterprise seeks to structure itself to facilitate collaboration among key functions, such as R&D, engineering, manufacturing, marketing, sales, and finance, its ability and agility to partner with customers and other partners for collective success can become quite powerful. The use of matrix management to release the power of the horizontal organization toward attainment of key outcomes makes broad intellectual sense.

However, the authentic challenge of matrix management is less intellectual and conceptual than it is behavioral and cultural. Few executives have trouble understanding the architecture and logic of the matrix organization. The challenge is in exercising shifted roles and rules that are needed to lead and participate in a matrix of cross-functional teams pursuing mutual objectives using shared resources. Matrix management won't happen without planning and preparation. In addition, a host of changes need to be discussed face to face. Memos, PowerPoint slides, or e-mails alone won't cut it.

A genuine transition to matrix management will temporarily shake people out of their comfort zones, but if they are not outside of their comfort zones, then you are not really achieving change. What are some of the comforts that are left behind? What kinds of shifts in employee behavior and approaches become necessary in a matrix? The following shifts are specifically applicable to the matrix interface staff:

- Satisfying not only your functional supervisor, but also your horizontal matrix team leader and team members drawn from other functions.

- Relating to "unfamiliars" drawn from other functions whose values, perspectives, education, and experience may well differ from your own and the colleagues with whom you are accustomed to working.

- Focusing more on outcomes rather than on process or activities.

- Making decisions collaboratively to ensure that a mix of outcome *and* functional priorities are satisfied.

- Learning to span boundaries to work as well horizontally as you do vertically.

- Moving away from full reliance on formal, position-based authority and toward blending the power of expertise and the power of information into organizational life (where cross-disciplinary creative problem-solving, persuasion, and negotiation skills become increasingly important).

- Leaving the comfort of well-marked turf and responding to a persistent, driving emphasis on cross-cutting results – an emphasis that is driven by a horizontal matrix team leader who is accountable for goal attainment.

- Living with naked interdisciplinary transparency so that each function's contribution to the value proposition becomes more visible with each passing day.

These are significant shifts and it is important to talk about them and what they mean, particularly with respect to executive expectations regarding how things will change and how people's behavior will need to change. In addition, communication should preview the coaching, training, and supportive supervision that is going to assist employees in making these shifts. Each of these eight shifts is described later in this chapter in Step 3, the training and coaching context.

It could be argued that the biggest changes will be experienced by the **Vertical Functional Leader**, who must now share **decision making** that was previously almost autonomous. It is understandable that the Vertical Leader may perceive this sharing of **decision making** as a loss of status, authority, and control. As time goes by, the functional leader will begin to adapt, finding the new role not only tolerable, but also more stimulating. The complex people planning that must be done in the matrix is challenging indeed. Collaboration with other vertical and horizontal counterparts on key strategic issues places the functional leader at the crossroads of the organization.

It is self-evident that information is power. The functional leader typically finds that she or he has access to more information in the matrix than ever before and, over time, will have more opportunities to use this information with greater impact.

So what are the implications for planning and communication? The Vertical Functional Leader's sensitivities need to be appreciated. This person's initial sense of losing status, authority, and control needs to be counterbalanced with opportunities and messages that play up the positive aspects of the change and provide fresh opportunities for the functional leader to make positive contributions in the new structure.

The functional leader must learn to serve and to dictate. By way of functional service quality, the matrix demands a burden of proof that goes beyond that in the traditional hierarchy. The functional leader in the matrix has a burden of proving that the functional services being offered and delivered are the best available – in-house or outsourced. This challenge is made more difficult because, with the help of the matrix interface staff, the vertical leader must balance the volatile needs for service and support from different matrix teams, and avoid excessive peaks and valleys within the limits of human capability.

Planning and Preparation for Matrix Management in a Vertical Function

The Vertical Leader should draw together all of the function's matrix interface staff and ensure that these questions are explored and communicated to the appropriate personnel:

Questions to Pose to Matrix Interface Staff

❑ What questions do matrix interface staff have about their vertical role and responsibilities relative to their horizontal role and responsibilities?

❑ What do matrix interface staff members, drawn from the different matrix teams, expect of one another? How often should they meet? About what?

❑ What do matrix interface staff expect from the Vertical Leader?

❑ How can a matrix interface staff best uncover the need for a decision that affects the entire function?

❑ How can decisions be expedited within the function and then be communicated among all staff?

❑ How will major tensions and/or conflicts between any matrix team(s) and this function be resolved?

❑ What are short-term priorities common to all matrix interface staff regardless of the matrix team to which they are assigned?

❑ What are the short-term ways in which each interface staff member is expected to improve matrix team functioning?

❑ How will the functional unit's input best be integrated in the thinking of each matrix team?

Each of the **Horizontal Matrix Team Leaders** will have challenges as well. For one thing, as a fledgling matrix organization is implemented, typically you will find that the horizontal matrix team is chronically underpowered relative to the traditional vertical functions that have long existed in the organization, for instance, manufacturing, marketing/sales, etc. Powering up the horizontal teams, particularly in the beginning, takes some planning. The matrix teams need to be granted authority over some key decisions to overcome the temptation to bypass the new matrix structure in favor of the old way.

The Matrix Team Charter. **The key to understanding matrix management is in understanding the fundamental building block of the matrix organization – the cross-functional matrix team.** An early preparatory task is to establish a charter for each matrix team. The team charter defines what the team needs to do, why it is doing it, and how it is supposed to do it. The charter should be developed by the team members, probably with the aid of a facilitator, and should be documented and shared broadly.

An example team charter is displayed below drawn from a live example that worked for the company. The company's matrix teams were organized by customer segment.

The Matrix Team Charter

What to Do?

1. Establish a long-term vision for the sector and create a business plan to support the firm's goals and increase global profitability.
2. Manage the business plan.
3. Manage product requirements and sales and operational planning.

4. Ensure alignment of core functional teams with business plans.

5. Expand understanding of the entire business from a well-rounded perspective.

6. Recommend effective deployment of company assets.

Key Measures

In addition to the firm's scorecard, each matrix team has its own scorecard that charts progress according to the following areas:

1. Team Attainment of Key Results

2. Improvements in Speed to Market

3. Team Satisfaction Measures

4. Team Effectiveness Measures

Boundaries

1. Company liability, policy, safety, corporate controls, personnel decisions.

2. Prior consultation required for any change in process, materials, or other elements that impact the fixed cost structure.

Each matrix team should be in a unique position to make a significant difference by leveraging cross-functional synergy within its purview and by defining how company strategies apply in the team's purview and to the production function that manufactures products for its customer base. Specifically, the following advantages undergird the firm's organizational strategy:

1. Drive efficiency and cost reduction

2. Strengthen new product development

3. Upgrade resource management to achieve proper resource allocation and use

4. Achieve project prioritization and serve as priority-setting gatekeepers

5. Understand and incorporate cost of quality/warranties as relates to vendor performance to provide needed information

6. Strengthen interface among functions

7. Improve organizational capability in sales-operation planning.

How Do We Do It?

1. We attempt to resolve issues at the team level.

2. We use regular (one-on-ones, monthly, quarterly, etc.) review schedules.

3. We strive to achieve more intense, productive dialogue at business plan and quarterly updates.

4. We continuously improve our business planning and spell out specific action items for follow-up, milestones for review, and a quarterly check of long-range assumptions to determine if they remain valid.

5. We consistently and continuously communicate key intentions to top company staff, striving for over communication.

6. We access high-performing employees for business team (BT) projects and core BT initiatives.

7. We conduct a team self-assessment twice a year to assess team progress, to plan/replan, and to assess support from functional areas using a common framework.

8. We continuously improve our use of data in fact-based **decision making** and documentation, providing more detailed reports, meeting minutes,

and specifics on needs for additional or different support.

9. We involve the functional representatives actively throughout.

The establishment of horizontal power requires a blending of confidence and competence. The selection of matrix team leaders must be accomplished carefully and skillfully. Incapable matrix team leaders need to be replaced promptly: there should be a contingency plan for doing so.

The matrix team leader must cultivate empathy with matrix interface staff who are drawn from the functional areas and treat them as full-fledged team members rather than considering them "service providers" who report to someone else.

Part of the preparation of the matrix team leader is in building the understanding that bluster and threats are unacceptable as a way of prompting responsiveness in the organization. A mix of reason and advocacy is expected in the matrix. The challenge is to stand up for requirements without developing a fatal reputation for overstatement, false deadlines, and similar threat-based actions.

The matrix team leader is expected to search for imaginative ways to share resources with peers and not engaging in power plays and end runs. The promise of the matrix rests in part with the effectiveness of the matrix team leaders; planning and communications that strengthens their ability to pursue cross-functional goals are mandatory, not optional.

It is essential that there be role clarity concerning the responsibilities of the matrix team leader, consistent with the team charter. In other words, if the team charter is meaty and hearty, the role of the team leader will need to be correspondingly strong.

Drawing from the same case study that supplied the sample charter, a team leader definition is supplied below for example purposes only. While there are certainly other samples, this one fits well with the charter and with where the firm wanted to go with matrix teams.

Matrix Team Leader Responsibilities

1. Ensure team meets its goals
2. Facilitate collaboration and conflict resolution
3. Manage upwards and serve as conduit to senior staff
4. Build and promote team culture, generate excitement through strategic visioning, and celebrate successes
5. Exhibit long-term commitment to business
6. Keep team members focused and accountable
7. Apply excellent planning, communication, and meeting skills to coordinate meetings, activities, etc.
8. Develop and apply cross-functional knowledge ensuring that all disciplines have a balanced voice
9. Ensure inter-team communication
10. Lobby for needed resources, balancing team goals with other workloads
11. "Close the back doors and confiscate the keys," meaning defend vigorously the role of matrix teams in setting priorities and allocating resources to minimize organizational circumvention and resource siphoning
12. Take risks
13. Request human and other resources needed to fulfill team charter

Planning and Preparation for Matrix Management for the Horizontal Matrix Team

The Horizontal Matrix Team Leader should draw together all of the team's matrix interface staff and ensure that the following questions have been explored and communicated to the appropriate personnel:

- ❑ What are the key result areas (do-or-die goal sets) for our team and how will we know when we have achieved success?

- ❑ What are our top near-term priorities?

- ❑ What is the support to be given and support to be received from and between each of the team members?

Life in the matrix is especially challenging for the **Staff Interface Team Member** who resides at the intersection of the vertical and horizontal axes. A lot of hope and promise of the flattened, faster, resource-efficient matrix organization rests with these team members.

As with the team leader, it is important to clarify the role of the staff interface or matrix team members. Drawing once again from the previous case study, here are the role responsibilities that the firm set forth for matrix team members:

The Team Member

1. Develop and apply the ability to communicate and implement team plans within one's function

2. Support team goals/activities based on your function/area of expertise

3. Be assertive enough to represent your function effectively on your matrix team and expose applicable functional issue, e.g., skills resources, timing that relate to goal accomplishment, and education of others on your functional objectives

4. Serve as your team's primary interface with your function head

5. Contribute to goals and objectives with dedicated commitment; pull weight and follow through

6. Share responsibilities and promote team consensus

7. Exhibit willingness to challenge and to be challenged by other team members

8. Cultivate team integrity and trust, and build the strength of the team by controlling functional pre-reads and pre-edicts prior to the development of the matrix team's comprehensive, cross-functional strategy

9. Exhibit long-term commitment

The staff interface serves on the horizontal team and also as a member of a vertical or functional team of his counterparts on other matrix teams. She or he may serve as staff interface on more than one matrix team if staffing constraints make this necessary.

The staff interface is responsible for communicating proactively – vertically, horizontally, and diagonally. She or he must avoid absolutes and cultivate alternative viewpoints to negotiate trade-offs. The staff interface must vet issues throughout the organization rather than expecting "the boss" to work through the organizational politics. A key mandate is that the staff interface is able to resolve complex issues faster on a multidisciplinary, i.e., cross-functional, basis and do so at the lowest possible organizational level.

What are the new skill implications for the staff interface within the matrix? The ability to win support on key issues and yield on less critical points.

Planning and Preparation for Matrix Management for the Effective Staff Interface

There is great usefulness in each staff interface sitting down with the Vertical Leader and the Horizontal Matrix Leader in a brief huddle to explore some of the basic questions of how the matrix will function:

- ❑ Who performs what work? Who makes what decisions? With whom must she or he consult?

- ❑ What is to be done?

- ❑ Why is certain work to be done? What is the contribution of that work to goal attainment and/or customer satisfaction?

- ❑ Where is the work to be done?

- ❑ When is the work to be done? How are deadlines to be set? What is to be done when Matrix Team and Vertical Function timelines are out of sync or in conflict?

- ❑ How is the work to be performed, i.e., with what methods or procedures? Are there specific quality requirements or unique imperatives that need to be satisfied?

Planning and Preparation for Matrix Management By and For Top Leadership

Top leadership should communicate to all employees who will be involved with or affected by the move to matrix management – that it will do a "matrix management check-up" periodically to ensure that problems are averted. Leadership should share the check-up questions, such as those listed here, in advance with all parties concerned.

- ❑ Are different organizational components able to work with one another and respect each other's prerogatives using the Basic Matrix Role Dichotomy?

- ❏ Is there recognition of interdependence and how this interdependence can be leveraged?

- ❏ Have roles and responsibilities been clarified for each individual?

- ❏ Are key executive messages surrounding needed cultural changes getting repeated and getting through?

- ❏ Are quick hits of success resulting from new synergy being identified and communicated widely?

- ❏ Does each individual understand his or her annual objectives?

- ❏ Is there a willingness of staff and leaders to share information transparently and to work collaboratively with one another?

- ❏ Is communication among team members strong and getting stronger?

- ❏ Are there progressive improvements in understanding the benefits of matrix management and are those benefits being achieved?

- ❏ Are improvements occurring in the speed and quality of employee learning?

- ❏ Is the Basic Matrix Role Dichotomy structure working for everyone? If there are difficulties, what are they and how can they be resolved?

Step 3: Lead and Train Your People

Executive behavior during matrix management implementation is keenly important. Executives can easily lose sight of their own importance and forget that employees often hang on their every word. Managers and staff then go on to interpret, misinterpret, and repeat what the executive said. I coach executives to envision themselves wearing a broadcast headset that cannot be removed; they should never utter words that they don't want others to hear over the company-wide loudspeaker or see as the headline in the company newsletter.

Advice to the Executive

Executives should be particularly reflective and circumspect during a time of structural change. Here are some suggestions:

1. Think before you speak and, when possible, vet significant thoughts with your trusted inner circle and with other influential peers.

2. Share your impatience with the rate of progress, but keep the most discouraging thoughts to yourself. Remember, the benefits of the matrix are hard-won; don't let the daily frustrations knock the entire enterprise off stride.

3. Don't waffle in public – stay the course. Do not depart from your reorganization design or institute a mid-course modification until the implementation of the new organization is given a fair chance to succeed. Don't talk about modifications until you are poised to act promptly.

4. Consider the context in which your words will be heard and understood. Remember that it is your job to lead the reorganization "caravan," even to the point where the vehicles in the entourage can barely make out your taillights. Communicate with members of your organization in the context of what they are currently working on, giving them glimpses of the future you see, but without distracting them from their current vantage point.

5. Remember that there is a big, big difference between thinking something, or even saying something, and having it realized. The job of the executive is highly cerebral, but don't confuse intellectual richness with the craggy shoals of day-to-day reality. The fact that your inner circle is on the same wavelength as you provides no guarantee that subordinate managers and staff have a clue as to what you think or want.

6. Set some inspection targets and then make these inspections – without fail. Announce in advance what your inspection punch list will be. Questions such as those listed earlier in this section may provide guidance. Indicate that you will randomly communicate with participating staff to learn how clearly and confidently they can respond about how the new organization works. But this is not a quiz show: Everyone should know what the questions will be in advance.

7. Human resources people should wade into the middle of your matrix organization. Implementation of structural change is both an air war and a ground war. You cannot achieve structural change using strictly an air war of all-hands meetings, memos, newsletters, executive videolinks, and the like. These are important for setting the stage and communicating the tone, but on-the-ground action by your management team and by HR managers and staff is essential. In the near term, HR staff and/or a contracted consultant should provide training, facilitation, and focus-group support during implementation. They should also be involved in furthering matrix systems, leadership, and culture change on a longer-term basis. Your HR people can and should be the folks who help your employees make sense out of change. They should help employees mourn the past and celebrate the new to expedite organizational transition.

HR Support During Implementation

Human resources can support matrix management implementation through training, facilitation, the conduct of focus groups, and other activities.

Training. Implementation should be accomplished through a training program of some length. Depending on the number and ability of involved staff, a half-day, one-day, or even two-day session may be needed. At the conclusion of the training, each participant should be able to accomplish these tasks:

- ❑ Define an effective matrix organization in terms of desired success factors, evolutionary stages of development, and self-appraisal metrics

- ❑ Identify issues and potential pitfalls that must be managed to minimize implementation problems

- ❑ Use tools and techniques to clarify responsibility and authority, resolve differences, and correct ambiguity.

In addition, participants should exit the training conversant in these, more detailed, topics:

1. Understand and be able to explain matrix management

2. Describe how the principle of a person reporting to only one supervisor is applied in a matrix

3. Understand and be able to explain several advantages of the matrix form

4. Identify changes that the vertical organization will experience

5. Identify changes that the horizontal organization will experience

6. Understand and be able to explain potential matrix pitfalls and how to avoid them

7. Understand and be able to explain how an effective matrix functions

8. Identify the stages of team formation

9. Describe effective meetings management in the matrix organization

10. Describe early matrix management implementation steps and their importance.

Shifts in Employee Behavior

Training, mentoring, coaching, and supportive supervision is also necessary to help matrix-impacted employees increase their interpersonal skills and confidence. This helps employees make the shifts that were mentioned in Step 2. The challenge is to equip, coach, and coax employees to try new things in new ways. Each of these shifts is described in additional detail below.

Shift 1: Satisfy Multiple "Masters": Not only your functional supervisor, but also your horizontal matrix team leader, along with matrix team members drawn from other functions

A functional supervisor who seeks to extend, or possibly retain, his or her hegemony over prerogatives that are assigned to the horizontal matrix team leader often complicates this challenge. Making this shift successful requires that the Basic Matrix Role Dichotomy be in full force and effect. In this way, the go-to person at the matrix interface has more than a fighting chance to satisfy both the functional supervisor and the matrix team leader.

However, the observance of the **Basic Matrix Role Dichotomy** is only one aspect of satisfying "multiple masters." Success also requires diplomacy on the part of the go-to person. This most often means "shuttle diplomacy" between the vertical and horizontal leaders so that collaboration provides final authority for decision making to the appropriate leader based on the nature of the decision, but also encourages the consultation and buy-in needed for continued working harmony, even in the face of material disagreements.

For the go-to person, the challenge is to persuade and negotiate rather than to simply wait for things to be resolved from "on high." This sometimes means that the go-to person calls a meeting with the functional and matrix team leaders to expose dueling priorities, conflicting objectives, or significant resource shortages. The go-to person is usually more accustomed to being summoned to a meeting rather than doing the summoning, and yet, the responsibility of the go-to person to be aggressive in calling such meetings with supervisors and other matrix team members is absolutely necessary to matrix management success. Timid go-to people will bring the matrix down!

Shift 2: Do Talk to Strangers: Relate to "unfamiliar" people drawn from other functions whose values, perspectives, education, and experience may well differ from your own, in addition to those of the colleagues with whom you are accustomed to working

This is the shift where the rule changes from "don't talk to strangers" to "*do* talk to strangers!"

For those who harbor "occupational prejudices," this shift will prove especially difficult. But what is an occupational prejudice? Think about a coworker who says things like, "I'll work with anyone except the lawyers," or, "If we need to work with the engineering staff, someone besides me ought to go talk with them."

Where do occupational prejudices come from? They may originate from a bad experience that the employee – or a relative or friend of the employee – had. It may be an experience that the employee can't recall consciously, but yet it has left a lasting stain that is an impediment to effective cross-functional relationships.

The best way to overcome any sort of prejudice and to grow trust and comfort in working with a different group of any kind is to dive in to the mix with them.

This discussion may seem so elementary that you wonder why these words appear on the page. If that's true, then good for you! However, please be mindful that others may be uneasy with interacting outside their functional comfort zone. You may need to coach them to change.

Part of this coaching involves educating the individual about the value that is added by each of the functions in the matrix. It is not safe to assume that everyone knows each component's contribution, be it legal, finance, R&D, or some other function. In addition, the interfaces between and among the functions that help us attain synergy may yet be unknown and unexploited.

Unease can also be caused when it is unclear how one function can help another function be fully successful. What kind of support do you need from me to be successful in making your contribution to the overall goal? Here's what I need from you in making my contribution successful. This type of conversation goes a long way toward establishing bonds of support, given and received. Only when the nature and extent of mutual support is known – and this web of support *is* the modern organizational network – can we develop informal protocols for sharing support that will strengthen interpersonal comfort and effectiveness.

Such understandings tend to evolve over time, but we don't have a lot of time to let these things play out organically. We also don't want to have these developments occur by happenstance. By training and coaching you can usher the process along with all due speed.

Shift 3: Adjust Your Focus Toward Outcomes: Focus more on outcomes rather than on process or activities

You might well proclaim, "What do you mean, focus more on outcomes? What do you think I've been doing?"

And I will respond, "Relax." No one is suggesting that you are not an outcomes-oriented person. On the other hand, are you focused on the highest priority outcomes for your organization? The idea that your priorities and your organization's priorities might be different can be fighting words in some circumstances, but these are issues that need to be explored in a matrix if the success factor of "objectives alignment" is to be attained.

Here's an example of what I'm talking about. When Madeleine Albright was Secretary of State, I was involved with a project to translate the U.S. government's *Strategic Plan for International Affairs* into strategic and operational plans for overseas missions, for major functional bureaus in the State Department, and for affiliated agencies, such as the U.S. Agency for International Development (AID), International Broadcast Bureau (Voice of America), and other offices. To use a broad generalization, the diplomatic corps has long been accustomed to what I characterize as "freelancing," meaning that it likes what it does and does what it likes. The reasoning of many freelancers is that the world is just too volatile to be tethered to plans and outcomes. These diplomats will talk about process and activities, arguing that eventually the outcomes of their efforts will be revealed. **Top executives must be clear and forceful in indicating that the focus must be on outcomes –** period. Otherwise, freelancing will abound and we may all be using walkers by the time results show themselves, if ever!

In another example, scientists employed in pharmaceutical R&D, as with most professionals, relish being recognized by peers at conferences, presenting papers, and networking. There is a strong business case to be made for encouraging such activities. However, if the outcome focus of the company changes in a direction that no longer supports the conference research projects that the scientist has made companionable with his "day job," we *may* have a problem. I say "may" because the company's pockets may be deep enough and the human resource management value hefty enough to warrant continued investment of company talent and infrastructure. On the other hand, as one COO put it plainly and directly, "We are in the business of discovering and developing new drugs – we are not in the conference-attendance and paper-presentation business."

In these and other cases the message is clear: Strike a balance. Without compensated outcomes, there are no activities and there is no process. On the other hand, without process and activities, there will be no outcomes. It's not either/or, it's both/and. Agility and flexibility are desired traits of the matrix organization. When desired outcomes change, the idea is that the matrix can adapt quickly, shift focus, and remix activities. In a matrix, this usually means "all hands on deck" – with everyone moving in the same direction rather than permitting freelancers to carry on as they please.

The matrix organization puts a giant spotlight on free-lancing activities with close-up surveillance by matrix interface team members. The matrix encourages continuous interrogation concerning what is adding value and how. If something is not adding value, it will stick out like the proverbial sore thumb before too long. To not address value depletion forthrightly is to invite morale problems and worse.

Shift 4: Make Decisions Collaboratively: Collaborative decision making ensures satisfaction of a mix of outcome *and* functional priorities

To amplify a point introduced earlier, I want to emphasize that the **Basic Matrix Role Dichotomy** defines final decision-making authority, but it does not define the decision-making process as such. In other words, the mere possession of decision authority does not imply the absence of extensive consultation or collaborative decision making – horizontally, vertically, and diagonally. Indeed, the nature and extent of leading, informing, consulting, and approving can be formalized using the LACI diagram, introduced in Chapter 3, but explained in detail in Chapter 5.

In both private and public organizations, I often witness a tendency to confuse "consultation" with "approval." Consultation and approval are two different things. I can consult with legal counsel and then proceed to ignore its advice. If I choose to ignore legal counsel, I do so at my own peril, but, in the final analysis, the decision is mine to make. I must choose which advice to heed and which advice to ignore based on circumstances, as I understand them and the results for which I am accountable. On the other hand, there are likely circumstances where legal counsel possesses actual "pre-approval" authority. If this is true, we need to define the scope of such pre-approval and differentiate it from areas that are truly non-binding consultation.

There are great advantages to be found in collaborative decision making so long as it is not used to dilute ac-countability. Collaboration permits us to learn from mistakes that others have already made or witnessed. It permits us to find a "third way," a better solution we may have not seen. We can achieve a higher degree of synergy and enthusiastic buy-in that will not only result in a better decision, but more importantly, a decision that is actually implemented!

Should there be collaboration for collaboration's sake? No one is advocating that, particularly given the speed of business today. However, collaboration where there is synergy, resource savings, breakthrough solutions, and a valid exchange of ideas – with rich and constructive disagreements – is well worth pursuing. Collaboration, in combination with strong, fast, and precise communication, is an important ingredient in the matrix management mix.

Shift 5: Span Boundaries: Learn to span boundaries so you can work as well horizontally as you do vertically

Most people work well and easily with supervisors and colleagues in their functional area. Folksy descriptions of this comfort level, such as "feels like home" or "fits like an old shoe," are pretty accurate. Some of us may be a bit more uncomfortable if not downright clumsy when we tread beyond the familiar into the realm of the accountants, the lawyers, the R&D people, the manufacturing people, or others with whom we need to collaborate cross-functionally in pursuit of team goals.

I have noticed over the years a special irony about matrix organizations. The logic of the matrix organization is particularly compelling in scientific and technical organizations where the possibilities of cross-disciplinary synergy, integrated science, and shared infrastructure seem virtually infinite. Yet, these are the very enterprises that tend to be populated by introverts who may have the greatest difficulty in spanning boundaries!

An engineering/construction company executive described the situation this way: "Our introverted engineers look at their shoes when they talk to you. The extroverts look at the other guy's shoes." And here I repeat my favorite example of the bench scientist at a biotech firm who said, "Listen, if I wanted to work with people, I wouldn't have become a scientist."

In implementing matrix management, there are two success factors that are routinely ignored, namely "staff interpersonal skills" and "staff confidence." It is unwise to leave these success factors to chance because they don't automatically improve. You can help apparent introverts spread their wings and span boundaries if you apply training, mentoring, coaching, and supportive supervision.

My experience is that motivated employees, no matter how introverted, will surprise you with what they can do if they come to understand that (1) boundary spanning is an expected part of job performance, and (2) they receive some tips and pointers about how to connect with other people in other disciplines. It should be obvious that I am not defining "connecting" as the mere exchange of e-mails; the connection should be in-person where possible, and by phone and videoconference when working virtually.

Shift 6: Enhance the power of expertise and information: The matrix moves us further away from full, strict reliance on formal, position-based authority and toward blending the power of expertise and the power of information into organizational life – cross-disciplinary problem-solving, persuasion, and negotiation skills become increasingly important

The FBI is one organization that has been militant in its resistance to leaving 20th century stovepiped authority based on formal position power, so don't expect matrix management to work well there. Presidents, Congress, and all manner of FBI directors have tried to rectify the problems created by the FBI's failure to share information – including in the pre-Sept. 11, 2001, period, on Zacarias Moussaoui, the so-called "20th hijacker" – only to see reform efforts rebuffed, scuttled, or hopelessly delayed.

The good news is that most of us don't work in calcified or fossilized organizations. For instance, scientific and technical companies or agencies have hierarchies, but they have long had the power of expertise and information flowing through their veins. Formal position-based authority remains important. It's just that today's organizations have a need to blend various types of power in a mix to shape the present and future.

As organizations become more networked and less rigid in their hierarchies, employees will be able to wield the power of expertise and the power of information with greater skill and potency. To do so, however, will require sharpened presentation skills. It will also challenge technical people to do what they find counterintuitive – summarizing mountains of technical detail in to hard-driving executive headlines. Finally, the ability to persuade and negotiate will prove increasingly important, creating the need for training assistance.

Shift 7: Emphasize Cross-Cutting Results: Leave the comfort of well-marked turf and respond to the persistent, driving emphasis on cross-cutting results – an emphasis that is driven by a Horizontal Matrix Team Leader who is accountable for goal attainment

The matrix team leader's insistent emphasis on cross-cutting results will, when operating at full force, nudge the go-to person out of the comfort zone. The go-to person at the interface will need to rally leaders and staff at the home function to bend and flex in the direction required by the matrix team for the attainment of team results.

The matrix team-driven horizontal pressure for goal attainment prompts the go-to staff interface person to press his or her functional unit to deliver faster/better/cheaper, and in a manner customized to the needs of the matrix team's assigned marketplace or goal set.

This insistent focus on results causes the go-to interface player to move beyond roles of "coordinator," "collaborator," or, pejoratively, "protoplasmic message system," and into the role of "double agent," or better yet *agent provocateur* – an agitator for new connections, new support interfaces, new techniques, new approaches, and new talent.

This cross-cutting pressure means both the whole and the parts get supported. For example, in a marine fisheries research matrix, the collaboration between marine biologists and economists had not yet been developed and cultivated. Yet all marine science projects chronically face a threatening budgetary environment. Each project must demonstrate genuine value. One team is focused on a fish species whose population is small and declining. The challenge is to make a cogent argument for continuation of research on this species. Collaborating with the economists and showing the value that the species delivers to the entire ecosystem, particularly to more well-known and highly valued species that are important to commercial harvesting, serves both the interests of the whole and the needs of the individual team project. The matrix organization makes it easy to highlight the intersection between the species research matrix team and the go-to member for marine economics. It also simplifies the cross-functional collaboration needed to create a detailed budget plan and justification.

Shift 8: Increase the unmistakable visibility of each function's contribution: Live with naked interdisciplinary transparency so that each function's contribution to the value proposition becomes more visible with each passing day.

Did I say naked? There is a stark transparency that arises from the need to explain how a step performed by one function in a cross-functional process adds genuine value to the entire process and encourages the attainment of the matrix team's accountable outcomes. Why is it necessary to do that? How does doing that help bring us closer to our goal? These and other queries turn the spotlight on each function's independent and synergistic contribution to the value proposition. As time goes on and team members become more familiar with one another's methods and procedures, there will be increased appreciation and anticipation of what the other function needs and why. However, there will also be tougher questions about whether top value is being added when a particular activity or procedure is performed.

I recall an example from pharmaceutical R&D involving the biostatisticians. The regulatory affairs attorneys kept inquiring about why the biostatisticians were employing an approach or procedure that was not required by FDA guidelines. The pharmacologists and medical staff also perceived no added value. The cross-functional team was zeroing in on the procedure, insisting politely that the biostatisticians justify the added time and expense associated with their approach. Ultimately, this line of inquiry helped the biostatisticians adopt new economies!

These eight shifts have important implications for training, mentoring, coaching, and supportive supervision. To be sure, the degree to which these shifts require attention and the nature and extent of the attention should be diagnosed in the context of your particular organization.

Facilitation. Training is part of the solution, but not the whole answer. Facilitation that is combined with training, or that is provided as a follow up, is required to work through the Basic Matrix Role Dichotomy, Team Charter Development, Team Leader Role Definition, Team Member Role Definition, the LACI Diagram, and more.

Focus Groups. Using the "punch list" questions displayed under Step 2, as well as other questions of importance to your organization, consider conducting focus groups of influential people and high-performers, but also any staff members who are disgruntled. The participants should be assured that their perceptions and suggestions will be kept confidential, except that overall implications will be shared with management in an effort to identify future support needs and direction. Such focus groups generally run 60–90 minutes.

Other Support Activities. Systems, such as employee performance planning and evaluation, pay levels, job descriptions, and reporting patterns, must be modified to reflect and accommodate the matrix organization. Employee performance planning and evaluation should help sustain the delicate power balance between the horizontal and vertical axes. With each interface staff member's work being directed by two superiors in two different aspects, each supervisor should participate actively in the staff member's evaluation. To get the greatest value from the evaluation, it is recommended that both supervisors conduct a two-on-one evaluation with the employee, maintaining carefully the division between the respective sides of the basic matrix role dichotomy.

As mentioned previously, organizations implementing matrix management soon discover that there are critical success requirements. An important leadership challenge is to establish a sense of urgency about the need for cultural change and ensure that there is greater organizational discomfort in remaining embedded in past practices. At least three areas of cultural focus stand out:

❑ **Meetings Management** – Everyone needs to plan and conduct effective meetings as a matter of course. I have counseled people to walk out of egregiously unproductive meetings in a matrix organization to raise the bar in no uncertain terms. When I provided that advice in response to a participant's question and the firm's COO quite agreed, the audience was shocked! Communications is critical to success in all organizations and particularly in the matrix. Meetings need to have a clear purpose – to make decisions, to provide information, to help employees prepare – and a set of clear objectives and a timed agenda. The ideal is to organize participation so that topics involve everyone at the beginning and then "shed" participants progressively throughout the meeting until the final topic involves just a small handful of participants. This "upside-down triangle" agenda model for respecting and making the most of participants' time by releasing them from the meeting as soon as possible is particularly appropriate in the matrix.

- ❑ **Conflict Resolution** – One critical job of the leader is to reward those who bring conflict out in the open and attempt to resolve it constructively. The leader should isolate and admonish those who mask or defer conflicts.

- ❑ **Open Communications and Trust** – Most organizations have some amount of back-stabbing, double-dealing, and a "dirty" underbelly. Such legacies surely leave behind hurt feelings and complicate the formation of trust. As Anne Donnellon points out in her book, *Team Talk,* "There is no way for a group to develop a fabric of reliable interdependencies unless its individual members give expression to their dependency, even when this means depending on (trusting) that which has yet to be proved dependable … ." In other words, the leader needs to make it plain that trusting behavior will be demonstrated despite the absence of a rational foundation for displaying such behavior. This approach is based on solid psychology: *First, you change the behavior and then the changed attitudes will follow.* Leadership as supported by HR helps employees mourn the past and let go of apprehensions that are grounded in past experiences. It takes coaching. It takes repetition. It takes propagating success stories and rewarding achievement promptly and visibly.

Employees will not make a significant leap of faith without being led by example. They will play "wait and see" instead. The effective leader must draw the holdouts out in the open, concocting opportunities to experience success in the new organization and encouraging them to become advocates for the new emerging culture.

The end result is that everyone feels free to bring up issues and express views, knowing that they are going to need to trust others prior to actually having demonstrated their trustworthiness. Don't just put your toe in the water – dive in!

Step 4: Inspect and Correct Dysfunction

Even when there has been sound implementation planning, leadership, training, facilitation support, and other integrative efforts to smooth adoption of the matrix structure, there will be dysfunctions. These dysfunctions need to be detected and corrected early.

There are five major traps that can be avoided if detected early. The traps can occur in any order and are introduced as follows:

- ❑ The Bermuda Triangle
- ❑ Narcissism
- ❑ Herd Mentality
- ❑ Tug of War
- ❑ Layering

The Bermuda Triangle condition refers to the type of chaos that occurs in the earliest stages of implementing the matrix when roles and responsibilities are undefined. During these early stages, unsafe assumptions are often made about how "easy" it is to "will" reorganization into place.

The Bermuda Triangle syndrome is a bit of anarchy where individual employees often suffer work overload and dueling priorities. This tends to afflict the most talented and/or most motivated of the employees.

It is essential that the nature and extent of disorder be brought out and that potential solutions be debated in a spirited, but reasonable manner. Cure anarchy starting from where you are. Challenge people in the organization to define and explain their roles, responsibilities, and decision-making prerogatives clearly and confidently. Require them to explain to whom and from whom they receive support in the organization and to what end. These efforts will help the Bermuda Triangle recede and make organizational life more predictable, with fewer "mysterious disappearances" of work, decisions, and people.

Narcissism is defined by the organization getting too involved in internal relationships and processes at the expense of the outside world of customers and stakeholders. This danger is most acute in the early stages of matrix implementation.

For the individual employee, this syndrome is a sort of "process infatuation" throughout the organization and a growing, and too often accurate, perception that the enterprise is losing sight of the customer and the competitive marketplace.

Narcissism draws its enormous power from a lack of collective and individual willingness to challenge the value of endless analysis; the fear of being caught in a mistake, no matter how minor or trivial, causes many people to get stuck in the web of analysis paralysis. One process attaches to yet another and the desire to find the "perfect order" within and among all of these individual processes takes over. The philosopher Voltaire provides an antidote with his maxim, "the perfect is the enemy of the good" – a good plan executed now is better than a perfect plan executed next year or never. Top leadership needs to discourage impossible perfectionism and to reward pragmatism.

Herd Mentality refers to a syndrome whereby everyone has to be involved in everything all of the time. This may be evidenced by a cast-of-thousands attendance at meetings or by e-mail cc: lists that are the size of the

Cleveland phone directory. As with the other dysfunctions, the herd mentality is yet another direct consequence of failing to adequately specify roles and responsibilities where everyone feels that the safe career bet is to attend virtually everything – to see and be seen at all times, regardless of value added. After all, they may reason, one's importance and contribution is up for daily definition when ongoing accountability is so vague and fleeting. Therefore, attendance at meetings becomes critical in the event that an opportunity to create or assert a role might present itself.

In this trap, everyone tends to get involved in every decision with Kumbaya-style consensus building, often involving inappropriate players whose expertise doesn't apply to the issue at hand. Herd mentality draws its enormous power from the individual's fear of separation from the group. Of special importance to matrix implementation is the fact that during times of change and ambiguity, the herding instinct is even more pronounced.

While there are many decisions that should be made in groups, not every decision is appropriate for group process. Enormous amounts of time can be wasted when there is a fundamental lack of preparedness to accept responsibility for actions.

Sometimes people complain that the implementation of matrix management means "there are more meetings than ever now that we are in the matrix." Closer examination often reveals that there were just as many meetings prior to implementing the matrix but that the "reorganization" becomes the Velcro for attaching longstanding traditions of insufficient meetings management.

Sometimes functional leaders who have traditionally enjoyed full decision-making authority resist the change to matrix management. They do this by intruding on decisions that are the prerogative of the horizontal matrix team leader. This can delay decision making and, in extreme cases, call the viability of matrix management into question or sabotage it. Leaders must remember the Basic Matrix Role Dichotomy and insist that it be used to govern who makes the final decisions. This is not to say that there should not be consultation between vertical and horizontal leaders prior to making a decision. It means that someone needs to be accountable and that the Dichotomy serves as the rule of engagement for making final decisions. Top leaders serve as referees and must call "offsides" when someone seeks to function outside of his/her given matrix role.

Curing the herd mentality requires strong medicine. It requires no-nonsense insistence on effective meeting planning and implementation, particularly in identifying participants and the value that is expected from their participation. It is not enough to use these antidotes just at the top or just at the bottom of the organization. Effective meetings and clear definitions of responsibility must exist throughout to escape the herd mentality's powerful grip.

Tug of War refers to the shifting balance of power. The price of agility is "instability." Not convinced? Think about this: A fossilized organization is stable, but it is far from agile. Matrix management is usually adopted because it provides for rapid response to changing external and internal conditions.

The tugs of war in organizational power struggles are not all bad. Indeed, such struggles can be helpful and an expression of constructive tension, particularly in a matrix. However, there is a governing principle: To win power absolutely is to lose performance ultimately. Tugs of war for resources need to be more frequent and less dramatic rather than less frequent and of high magnitude and impact. Power in a matrix involves flexible and near-constant negotiation, with top management serving as the final arbiter when absolutely necessary.

Tugs of war are a form of political expression. Politics arise when there is a greater demand for a resource than there is supply. Bringing rational, fact-based methods to bear is the best way to resolve an internal power struggle. Also, the Basic Matrix Role Dichotomy spells out who should decide what issues and it is important to use the Dichotomy in contentious situations. A step-by-step process is recommended, namely:

1. *Full understanding of the facts:* Reach full understanding of the facts behind the conflict

2. *Reach agreement:* Reach agreement on the issues that are involved

3. *Consider the "big" picture:* Consider the organizational impact of the conflict resolution

4. *Consider alternatives:* Consider the alternatives and their expected costs and benefits

5. *Strive for consensus but don't be paralyzed by the quest for consensus:* Resolve problems using a consensus-based decision process wherever possible but if consensus is impossible then make a recommendation, appending the minority opinion to senior management for final resolution.

Layering occurs when matrices develop within the matrix, going down through several layers of organization. My people's people will talk with your people's people! This may occur when an interface is populated by several, possibly a dozen staff, who have support roles to play that don't fit cleanly into the matrix team, particularly in its horizontal aspect. This creates confusion about when a matrix is not a matrix. It spreads doubt about when an interface team member is neither a full-fledged member of the horizontal, nor on the vertical team. Layering creates communication requirements with which no human being can possibly keep pace.

The antidote to layering is to require that each matrix team identify an individual team member along the horizontal and vertical axes, meaning that each staff interface is a unique individual. Matrix management is intended to make it *easier* to find "go-to" people rather than more difficult!

Matrix Analysis and Diagnosis

In the words of one COO: "It's easy, if there is any conflict between the vertical and the horizontal, the horizontal prevails. Period. Why? The answer is because revenue flows horizontally and expenses flow vertically. In my book, revenue always trumps expenses." The COO was responding to a question posed to him by one of his key executives as to who should prevail in the event of vertical-horizontal disagreement.

He answered before I could intervene. Later, I indicated privately that the preferred answer is that "it all depends." It depends on what type of issue it is and who has the final power to resolve it in accordance with the Basic Matrix Role Dichotomy. As a brief aside, he was correct that revenue flows horizontally and that expenses flow vertically in a matrix organization.

Achieving a healthy and constructive tension between vertical and horizontal elements is critical to achieving key benefits of speed, capacity utilization, goal focus, etc. The COO was on the right track in attempting to create overarching guidance that managers and staff can use in resolving conflicts. However, the guidance was too imprecise and, if followed, would lead to the vertical organization fading away, resulting in a new hierarchical structure – one laid on its side!

We do not want to substitute a horizontal organization for the previous vertical hierarchy. We don't want to return to a stovepiped organization, this time with stovepipes laid on their sides! To do so would *not* be matrix management.

Common Matrix Management Tensions

Three major types of matrix tension emerge from time to time:

- ❑ Interteam Tension
- ❑ Interfunction Tension
- ❑ Complex Tension

Interteam tension is evidenced by competition for financial resources, human talent, executive attention and action, equipment, deferral of expectations concerning return on investment, and so forth. Such tension can be caused by "drift-and-shift," e.g., shifting priorities in the organization, product launch delays, or other slipped deadlines, which threaten the most well thought out plans. Tensions can be caused by perceptions of differing levels of a function's support to one matrix team over another matrix team. Personality conflicts among matrix team leaders can prompt strife that has ramifications for team members as well as team leaders.

Interfunction tension is similar to interteam tension in symptoms, except that tensions between functions often are evidenced on various, but not necessarily all, horizontal teams.

When there are interteam as well as interfunction tensions, we can call it complex tension and know that diagnosis and correction of these tensions will be more intricate and time-consuming. If the teams are competing for scarce resources in more than one function and scheduling problems are emerging among teams and among functions as well, this can degenerate into complex tension in a matrix organization.

A Concluding Thought

This is the chapter that fleshes out the notion that methodical thought and action leads to matrix management success, rather than approaches dependent on wishing, hoping, hand wringing, and magical incantations.

If you pursue the four major steps in the spirit of ready-aim-fire, you will find that the wrinkles associated with managing matrix management structure and behavior can be isolated and eliminated. In addition, your matrix organization will be powered by constructive tension between the vertical and the horizontal rather than the dysfunctional forces of interteam, interfunction, and complex tensions.

CHAPTER 5:

Matrix Decision-Making and Action

Matrix roles and rules of engagement come together in the LACI diagram. This valuable tool clarifies who is involved with what decisions. I highly recommend that it be used at the outset of matrix management implementation. Thereafter, LACI provides the tabletop platform – for new teams with new challenges – that defines the responsibility of each member of the matrix.

LACI is an acronym that refers to:

L = **L**ead, which means *initiate and be responsible for the result*

A = **A**pprove, which means *responsible for result, but does not initiate*

C = **C**onsult, *where the consultation is on a meaningful level of exchange*

I = **I**nform, *where the responsibility is to keep everyone "in the loop"*

A sample LACI diagram is displayed on the next page. The rows and columns of the diagram are explained below:

❑ *Member Responsibility.* In this row, identify the key players involved, including horizontal matrix team leader, interface team members, vertical leader(s), COO or other top executives as appropriate, and other relevant entities.

❑ *Function/Task/Activity.* In these columns, you'll want to enter a major element of a core process. It might be a step-by-step sequence associated with a project, with the development of a product or with the selling of a service, or some A-to-Z process such as:

- Process and acquire customer
- Design solution
- Install solution
- Assure solution quality
- Bill and collect
- Follow-up for add-on customer service

LACI Diagram

LACI Diagram Worksheet

Team: Climate Goal
Date: 5/15/2007
Process: Program Phase, PPBES

L = Lead (initiator/Responsible for result)
A = Approve (Responsible for result, but doesn't initiate)
C = Consult (To be Consulted/meaningful level of exchange)
I = Inform (Keep everyone in the loop)
*Lower case letters indicate lesser degree of involvement

Function/Task/Activity: Step-by-Step							
	1	2	3	4	5	6	7
	Distribution of shell program plan (last year's) (9/17)	Analyze guidance (9/27)	Priorities discussion with climate board (to evaluate fiscal guidance) (09/24)	Adjust FY07 program plan to be consistent with priorities discussion	Internal/ external review of draft plan (10/11/07)	Revise and submit program plan (10/25/07)	Approval of program plan
Goal Team Lead/PM/MM	L	L	L	A	L	A	C
Component Leads	I	C	a	C/a		I	I
Project Managers	I	I	C/I			I	I
LO (AA)				I	C	I	I
Other goal / SubGoal Team Leads				C	C	I	I
Councils				C	I	I	I
Budget Officers				C	I	I	I
NEP/NEC							A
PPI						I	C
PAE						I	L
External Advisory					C		I

(Responsibility)

- *Enter L, A, C, or I* in Cell. Interrogate through each major function/task/activity and ask these questions:

  - Who needs to **Lead** this function/task/activity? In other words, who initiates or sparks activity when it comes to this step or function?

- Who needs to **Approve**? In other words, who is responsible for the result? Whose phone is going to ring if things go wrong? The assignment of the "A" for "approval" is often a contentious discussion. There are stages of approval, starting with pre-approval. The temptation is to assign several "A's" for approval to several people. This is a big mistake and is to be avoided at all costs! If there are pre-approval steps, then add to the steps displayed on the LACI diagram. If there is just one pre-approval en route to final approval, I suggest using a lowercase "a" for pre-approval entered in the cell of the responsible pre-approver, and an uppercase "A" for final approval. Beyond that level of compromise, the facilitator should insist on identifying additional steps so that approval authority is crystal-clear.

- Who needs to be **Consulted?** What people really mean when they say that multiple people need to "approve" something is that these people need to be meaningfully consulted prior to final approval. In other words, who do you want to touch base with before the final decision is made? Not all levels of consultation are created equal. In that spirit, I recommend the use of a lowercase "c" for perfunctory, largely routine consultation where the approving individual can "take or leave" the consultee's advice. I recommend an uppercase "C" for consultation where the burden is virtually on the approving individual to make the case for why she or he would ignore the consultee's advice. A decision to ignore the advice of legal counsel where LACI spells out an uppercase "C" would be a good example of a situation where, in most organizations, the approving individual would need to explain why she or he ignored counsel's advice.

- Who needs to be **Informed?** Who needs to know about what is happening and when so they can do their job most effectively? My experience is that sometimes it is assumed that someone wants to be consulted when they really have bigger fish to fry and only want to be informed. As with all of the letters in the LACI alphabet, the best way to discover the right rules that go with all of the roles is for all of the involved employees to work them out together through discussion.

Suggestions for Using LACI

The best way to complete a LACI diagram is through a facilitated conversation. After the facilitator has explained LACI and how it works, the next task is to identify the steps or functions to be diagrammed. The facilitator should emphasize to the group that some steps might be deleted or added as the conversation proceeds. For example, additional steps may be needed when a broadly described step contains an unworkable number of approvals.

When first using LACI, the tendency of groups is to make multiple entries of L, A, C, and I in a single cell that defines the intersection between a role and, say, a step. If this is the case, it usually means that you have not defined the function/task/activity with enough specificity, requiring a return to the drawing board to achieve a more precise definition of function/task/activity. Multiple entries may also mean that you have not yet sufficiently refined the role to be played by a given team member.

There may be a few examples of combined letters, e.g., L/A, for unique steps or organizational circumstances, but there should not be many.

The therapy of LACI is to be found in the conversation – the discussion and the debate – that leads to the identification of steps, the identification of roles, and the defining of their intersection using L, A, C, or I. The conversation can be frustrating and can get bogged down. However, the investment is well worth it. Plus, once the team has "LACI'd" a particular core process, the LACI patterns already defined will usually inform the effort to LACI the next process or set of tasks.

The purpose of LACI is to give the team's members a better sense of their roles and the rules of engagement surrounding these roles. It's a game plan the team uses to accomplish its mission. It helps players avoid stepping on toes, but doesn't burden them with information they can't use, won't use, or just plain don't want. LACI helps identify the right people to involve productively in consultation, by simply informing them or involving them in decision making. It helps players get a better sense of how they can constructively work together in a matrix way and, as such, it builds team member confidence – one of the factors critical to matrix management success.

The greatest usefulness of LACI diagramming is when the team is first being formed and is developing its roles, relationships, and approaches. What was at first a matter of discussion and negotiation becomes a useful habit over time. LACI also comes in handy when a team is faced with a new challenge and needs to implement new steps or new core processes. At these junctures, the team should display a poster-size Excel spreadsheet on the wall, or project the LACI diagram from your laptop, and then walk through the LACI process with all members participating actively and enthusiastically.

A Concluding Thought

Clients often hope for a series of cut-and-dried matrix management tools that can be loaded into a web-enabled toolkit for all to use. In my experience, the best matrix management "tools" tend to be checklists – some of which have been included in this book. The LACI diagram, however, is a genuine, fundamental, and powerful tool for matrix management. It is difficult if not impossible to enjoy the benefits of a matrix organization without using LACI, mainly because it marries and clarifies role and process definitions with little or no ambiguity.

CHAPTER 6:

The Multicultural Matrix

The challenge of matrix management is more complicated for global organizations than for domestic ones.
This is true even above and beyond the complexities of
using virtual, cross-functional teams whose members are
spread across the world.

A central challenge in implementing a global matrix is to
accommodate the mix of cultures represented by all the
different employees. Italians might behave somewhat
differently from the Swiss in a given situation. The French
might do things differently from our friends from India.
And so it goes. Cultures can't be ignored or suppressed,
but must be factored into matrix management design and
implementation strategies.

The immediate relevance of culture to matrix implementation relates to roles, rules, and authority. For example,
some cultures emphasize "who you are" vs. "what you
do." Matrix implementation is more complicated in these
environments because the matrix is not about the formal
trappings of status. Other cultures imbue a great deal of
meaning in formal authority and hierarchy. The unleashing of the horizontal organization in circumstances where
rigid hierarchies prevail will require some special attention – special training and coaching in how traditional
notions of hierarchy are altered when using matrix
management.

Still other cultures favor indirect, rather than direct,
communication. In these cases, expect a greater degree
of challenge in implementing the matrix, which relies on
direct communication as its driving force.

While it's hardly easy to predict all the different cultural mores that will be encountered by the matrix, there are some core variables that can be mixed and matched to come up with a description that fits almost any culture. The following variables provide a starting point for the "culture" discussion:

- **How time is viewed**: Is time viewed as highly structured or highly flexible, or something in between?

- **How relationships are viewed**: Do relationships trump rules or do rules trump relationships, or something in between?

- **How status is obtained**: Is status ascribed or achieved? Is status about who one is by birthright or is about one's credentials and what one can do? Or, is it something in between?

- **How the individual and the group relate**: Are individual rights more important than group duties? Are group duties more important than individual rights? Or, is it something in between?

- **How communication occurs**: Is communication direct? Is it indirect? Or, is it something in between, depending on the topic?

These cultural factors will affect several of the matrix management success factors introduced previously. The matrix management success factors are largely American or Western European constructs. When I talk about staff interpersonal skills and confidence needed for matrix management success, I should admit that these characteristics are being viewed through a Western, if not a just plain American, lens.

We can't assume that staff are going to "boundary-span," or seek to influence without authority, or call two superiors into a two-on-one meeting, or point out dueling priorities easily if they are coming from a culture where people communicate indirectly, respect their managers on the basis of inherited status, believe that relationships trump rules, or that individual rights supercede group duties.

Some cultures will be more amenable to matrix management than others. On the other hand, with time, patience, and meticulous effort, changes in behavior can mitigate cultural impediments so that every culture can learn to use matrix management effectively.

A Concluding Thought

There is ample business literature that provides excellent advice on how to manage in a multicultural context. There is no point in attempting to paraphrase that literature here. Suffice it to say that if your matrix organization is comprised of people and locations drawn from around the world, it is unsafe to assume that each and every culture is equally welcoming to matrix management and its attendant changes. Investigate the characteristics of each culture and develop pinpointed strategies for selling and facilitating implementation of key changes, being mindful that the forces that are driving you towards and restraining you from matrix management success will vary from culture to culture.

CHAPTER 7:

Hot Intersections: *Using the Matrix to Manage Attention – The Scarcest Resource*

Perhaps the scarcest of all resources in organizational and individual life today is *attention.* With so many tasks, gadgets, and other influencers competing for it, it is valuable to be able to gain and hold people's attention. In a sense, matrix management is about managing people's attention to particular issues at every level.

Issue importance in any organization varies over time, depending on changes in the customer, competitive, technological, financial, legal, and political environments, as well as on the basis of internal organizational dynamics. In a matrix, this means that all of the interfaces between horizontal teams and vertical functions are "not created equal." (Here I am not referring to the specific *employee* who functions at an interface, but instead to the *cross-cutting issues* that need to be matrix-managed at the structural interface or at the intersection between a goal team and a discipline, or between a customer team and a function.) You can display the relative importance of interfaces graphically. You can also stimulate important conversations, debates, and decisions using this technique and make it clear where leadership attention should be focused.

I group some specific interfaces as *"large and hot,"* requiring significant investment of attention and resources; others are categorized as *"small and cool,"* meaning that while they are significant, the interface is not highly critical. Finally, some interfaces are mere dots, indicating that they exist, but that they are not intrinsically rich in importance or significance because of the narrow nature of the relationship between a given horizontal team and function.

I previously introduced the graphic depiction of a matrix organization as an array of horizontal and vertical lines. Why? A straightforward overhead view of all of the interfaces (or intersections) among horizontal teams and functions permits the executive to clearly identify the following areas where:

- ❏ Considerable strategic importance abounds.

- ❏ Decision disturbances are expected, e.g., budgetary shortfalls, policy conflicts, dueling priorities, decision vacuums, groupthink, misaligned objectives.

- ❏ Operational challenges are likely, e.g., staffing problems, infrastructure constraints, shortages of particular specialists, laboratories, ships, planes, or plant capacity.

- ❏ Breakthrough opportunities for synergy and/or integration await exploitation.

- ❏ Substantive alignment areas, e.g., budgetary/programmatic alignment with headquarters and/or global corporate initiatives that present harmonious advantages.

Such considerations can be color-coded, such as red for strategic importance, orange for likely disturbances, yellow for expected challenges, and green for special opportunities. Color rings around each of the interface nodes can be "sized" – small or large – to show relative executive emphasis and to telegraph planned levels of executive surveillance and future review.

A client's regional chief scientific officer (CSO) recently pointed out the importance of the interface between a particular research program and the economic function/discipline in his organization. *Color that interface* **red** *and make it large!* By way of programmatic and budgetary justification, the initial cost-benefit analysis of this research program standing alone doesn't present well because of its relatively small annual dollar volume within the industry. However, when the research program is considered as the crucial accompaniment to an adjacent industry, its true value will become clear. A powerful and persuasive cost-benefit analysis will likely emerge, providing a striking analysis that can tell a different story altogether.

Such an analysis does not happen by accident; it must be made a matrix-managed priority and initiated. The executive clarifies the strategic intent that is meant both horizontally and vertically in the matrix organization, and then follows up to ensure that it's carried out, with direct consequences for failure. In this spirit, our CSO announced that the intersection of the research program with the economists is *"hot."* From this vantage point, he expects to see increased traffic around the core issues at that node. He has made it plain that he will not approve a plan that fails to produce evidence of collaboration between the research program lead scientist and the economists. He has every reason to expect success.

One point that I make in our *Matrix Immersion Training* is that the top executives leading the matrix organization are usually "of" the matrix, but not "in" it. By this we mean that the top executive – the Chief Operating Officer, Chief Marketing Officer, Chief Scientific Officer, for example – will lead and resource the matrix, using it as a tool to fulfill the organizational mission and to attain its goals, and, in that sense, is "of" the matrix. However, the lead executive sits atop the matrix and does not wear the jersey of a player within the matrix in the same way that horizontal team leaders, vertical functional leaders, and go-to interface persons do. In other words, matrix management should not be confused with participatory management, although there are times when matrix management can be highly participatory if the executive decides this is the best way to achieve results.

By scanning for and defining the nature of "hot" intersections, top executives who are "of" the matrix can communicate explicitly and productively with all of the players "in" the matrix. Specifically, the all-important matrix interface person (also called the "go-to" person, "team contact" or "vertical liaison") will have a more clear and confident sense of the issues that need to be planned and managed to achieve the victories ahead.

A Concluding Thought

Years ago, I used an excellent management training film in my seminars. Entitled "The Bolero," it conveyed the idea that the effective executive functions much like the conductor of a first-rate orchestra playing Ravel's classic work. Depending on the part of the musical score being played, each section of the orchestra be it strings, woodwinds, brass or percussion is either more or less important. In business the strategic and operational plans are the functional equivalent of the musical score. I like the idea that the executive who uses matrix management effectively can quickly identify and turn to the "first chair" who represents a particular function on a horizontal team when an opportunity or challenge develops. As it is in music, so it is in business: sometimes you're hot and sometimes you're not.

CHAPTER 8:

Cross-Functional Teams Coming Apart at the Seams? *Toward the Coherent Matrix Organization*

To help us see the way a coherent matrix òrganization might evolve in practice, let's create a fictional enterprise called *E-Markable*, and assume that it provides financial products and services to Wachovia, Bank of America, Washington Mutual, SunTrust, and others. *E-Markable* is a business that serves many different customers – each with their own wants and preferences – and is therefore challenged because each individual customer has certain expectations of how the company should fulfill *its* needs. To rise to this challenge, *E-Markable* has aligned its organizational structure according to customer-centered strategies and systems. This setup means that functional silos have disintegrated in favor of customer-focused teams staffed by personnel drawn from the various disciplines needed to deliver the comprehensive services that each customer expects.

In simple terms, the customer-paid revenue flows horizontally across each customer-focused team. Expenses incurred in earning the customer's revenue flow vertically down each functional discipline. The Horizontal (Customer-Focused) Matrix Team Leader is responsible for maximizing customer satisfaction and the profitability of her particular customer on behalf of the employer, *E-Markable*. The Vertical (Functional Discipline) Team Leader(s) is responsible for advancing the state-of-the-art products, setting policies and procedures in and for its discipline, attracting and developing staff talent, assuring quality control, and discharging other responsibilities that promote the definable *"E-Markable Way"* of doing business.

Sounds like a pretty good model, doesn't it? It is, except that there is a danger inherent in the arrangement established by our fictitious company, and by many companies in a host of industries. The danger is that a Customer-Focused Team, within a matrix or not, will drift off and become its own largely self-contained enterprise, with a set of policies and work processes that become increasingly unique to each customer. The risk over time is that fewer policies and work processes will be shared among the component teams of the organization, which may undermine the identity of *E-Markable* as a whole.

Some might reasonably ask: Is this really such a bad thing? Isn't this what being customer-focused is really about? The answer, once again, is that it all depends.

We could end up with a continuum where, at one end, all business units are cobbled together so tightly that each has few, if any, degrees of freedom. The other end of the continuum is where several definable companies live under the same roof, but share little in common with the rest of the organization – other than, perhaps, janitorial services. Big problems await companies that have developed such a fractured structure. At the one end, excessive splintering into customer-focused teams will usually result in several drawbacks, such as:

1. *Reductions of economies of scale.* The absence of shared policies and work processes will, over time, reduce the overall ability to share personnel, systems, plans, and other tasks designed to achieve economies of scale.

2. *Increased tension and diminished resources.* As interests, perspectives, and processes diverge, pressures to spin off as a separate company may mount, particularly among personnel who are assigned to a "winning" team – one that serves a customer with superior profitability and a hand-

some volume. In the interim, there will be other productivity-depleting, morale-sucking, talent-consuming tensions among customer teams of varying profitability that will complicate the harmonious alignment of objectives and resources over time. Such inter-team tensions typically complicate retention of talent for some teams and permit talent siphoning by others. This disruptive spiral can reduce a given team's potential for future growth. If the most profitable customer team actually spins off from the corporate entity, resources available for investment in growing existing customer teams, let alone for acquiring new customers, will diminish significantly. The departing, spun-off team will likely suffer significant disadvantage in negotiating with its single customer going forward, but live and learn!

3. *Increased expenses and decreased interteam cooperation.* Diminished opportunities to share policies, processes, and personnel will increase expenses and undermine the multi-team cooperation needed to acquire and service new customers, particularly fledgling customers whose growth potential is more long term.

Lost Opportunities

At the other, fractionated end, the company is totally driven by customers to the point that it has lost its own discernible identity. It becomes a "job shop" for its clients and thereby loses time, attention, money, and confidence -- attributes that are needed to gain competitive advantage through new enterprise-wide processes and technology. It may also be losing its ability to attract and cross-train superior staff talent. In our case study, the failure to define and develop an *"E-Markable* Way" pushes our company toward a differentiation strategy based on price. Whenever a company succumbs to competition on a "commodity" basis, it joins the "race to the bottom," also known as "How low can you go?" cost and price competition. At this point, the company may accelerate its outsourcing to other countries offering few, if any enforced environmental or labor standards. Innovation is driven by the needs and preferences of – who else? – the dominant customer. *E-Markable's* dominant customer may retain its position as a market leader and may continue to conduct increasing levels of business with *E-Markable,* with everyone living happily ever after. Or, the dominant customer may stumble for reasons that have nothing to do with the quality of *E-Markable's* product/service offering, jeopardizing the entire company. In that case, it becomes painfully clear that it was very dangerous for *E-Markable* to hitch its wagon too tightly to one entity.

So what are the implications for the matrix? If the horizontal customer-focused teams have become quite strong and the vertical functions meek, the matrix may implode if more and more of *E-Markable* is organized strictly around the dominant customer. As time progresses, there will likely be less and less regard for other customers. The idea of evolving a differentiable *"E-Markable* Way" will get tossed onto the scrapheap of history – joining other wild ideas held by "impractical people" who once worked there but no longer do!

In writing and speaking about matrix management, I often stress the need to power up the horizontal axis in a matrix organization. That's because, in the vast majority of organizations, the horizontal axis is what's new and different. It's the entity most often unfamiliar, unexplored, and chronically underpowered. The flip side, however, relates to the dangers of underpowering the vertical axis.

A company's emphasis on customer-centered and customer-responsive approaches can, it seems, be overdone. First, customer service means *service*, not *servitude*. Customer responsiveness is about *response* and blurring together with your customer to ensure that customer's business success – not the *erasure* of your corporate identity. Managing customer perceptions to achieve satisfaction requires setting expectations, and showing your customer how to achieve extraordinary results and value from full use of your services and products.

A complete blurring of a customer-focused matrix team into a mere extension of the customer's staffing can obscure the present and future advantages of your company remaining a coherent whole. Such a perversion can thwart the benefits that a well- designed, well-managed, and yes, customer-centered matrix organization bring.

Customer-focused matrix teams are an idea whose time has definitely come. However, once again, implementation must be accomplished through thoughtful care and with precision.

Customer-focused teams need to be integrated into the fabric of your one-company corporate way so that tailoring to the customer becomes a variation on a theme rather than a separate theme altogether. Absent an adequate vertical definition in your matrix, a customer-focused team being bullied by a dominant customer can burst your first-rate company. There are healthy, sustainable alternatives that matrix management can deliver if you rebalance the horizontal and vertical to avoid coming apart at the seams.

Specifically, you may wish to consider powering up your vertical functions so that you can stay ahead of the competition and, simultaneously, stay ahead of your dominant customer or customers.

It is essential to provide some level of research and development support to each technical discipline so that you are leading the customer and are not always "filling orders." The bolstered R&D capability needs to be amplified by marketing and sales efforts that cause the dominant customer to, in a sense, respect your company "for its mind." This strengthens the hand of your horizontal team to offer solutions rather than merely taking directions. Your company needs to be able to convince the customer that your way is better or that the way that your customer seeks to prescribe for you was your way already! You become a partner with the customer in solving problems rather than just another disposable vendor. In his 1996 book, *Sales Shock!* author Mack Hanan both predicted and described the end of selling products and the rise of comanaging customers. This now-classic book should be recommended reading for those companies that want to master the skills and approaches that are needed to prevent their cross-functional teams from splintering.

A Concluding Thought

Customer-focused cross-functional teams are a powerful structure for implementing close-to-the-customer strategies. The advantages of integrated selling increase the ability to not only satisfy customer needs and preferences but actually *anticipate* them and, in a sense, lead the customer to the next frontier, rather than *vice versa*. That's the promise of customer-focused matrix management. The danger is that the customer-focused matrix team will degenerate into a "job shop," for the customer, thereby detracting from one-firm synergy and from the advantages of a diverse customer base and investment in cultivating existing and new customers to avoid the perils of "putting all of the eggs in one basket."

CHAPTER 9:

Challenges of the Global Matrix and Virtual Teams

A virtual team is comprised of team members who share responsibility for turning out defined work and for achieving defined objectives, all from a flexible mix of stationary, mobile, and/or remote work environments.

A *cross-functional* virtual team has the characteristics of any virtual team, except that members are drawn from a spectrum of disciplines, collaborating in an orchestrated effort to achieve goals, provide customer satisfaction, etc. A cross-functional virtual team may be located in a larger matrix of cross-functional teams, where many of these teams are non-virtual or only partly virtual, perhaps for a specialized function or two.

Defogging the Virtual Team

There are plenty of virtual/non-virtual combinations, and plenty of opportunities for befuddlement in need of clarification.

A recent client asked me how to manage a "global matrix comprised of virtual teams." A *global matrix comprised of virtual teams* sounds a bit intimidating. However, the principles of effective matrix management that apply to cross-functional teams located on the same corporate campus or on several corporate campuses also apply to a global matrix with members arrayed in virtual teams that connect in something like a cyber web. In fact, the key problem needing attention was not related to the team's "virtuality," but was instead a classic matrix management syndrome that would create conflict and confusion whether it happened down the hall or on another continent.

The key difference with managing a global matrix comprised of virtual cross-functional teams vs. those teams that are collocated is that roles and rules must be *even more* clear; "adequate" roles and rules may be OK if team members work face to face, but they must be finely tuned if teams are going to interact well from remote locations.

The very technologies that make the virtual team possible – interactive videoconferencing, cell phone, e-mail, voicemail, fax machines, overnight packages, etc. – play a central role in understanding the differences between virtual and conventional teams. Even with open, visible, and instantaneous information in a shared digital space that prompts cooperative action, employees cannot communicate as robustly with one another in virtual environments as they do in traditional offices. Body language, occasional hallway intercepts, and other communications that occur in a shared physical space can facilitate "sense making" in the organization. Spontaneous synergy, brainstorming chemistry, instant innovation – call the dynamic what you will – can spring from those "same-room" contacts, yielding better, faster, and superior results on complex issues, projects, or challenges. There's no guarantee that non-virtual collaboration will achieve superior results, but it *can*.

To determine your enterprise's challenges, ask yourself a few questions: What are limitations of the software (groupware) that can organize the brains and behaviors of your team members? Groupware has its limits when it comes to addressing the full range of interpersonal issues involved in managing successful teams, particularly cross-functional teams working on complex projects, products, or customers. Sometimes these limits don't really matter, but when they do, it's important to understand them.

Think about just one slice of the problem: team brain-storming. Same-room brainstorming can nurture trust and forgiveness among team members, enabling them to risk vocalizing some just plain bad ideas. E-mail leaves an electronic record of all ideas, good and bad. Therefore, employees working in cyberspace may refrain from conceptual risk-taking. In point of fact, groupware may lead to groupthink. Groupthink is perfect for some projects, product development, and customer services, but deadly for others. Stated differently, every job is not suited for a virtual team. The best way to forge ahead may be to concentrate brainstorming over a sustained period of, say, several days, through the face-to-face convening of your company's talent. This collaborative in-person effort may achieve markedly superior results compared with staccato off-again/on-again electronic meetings during which momentum and depth of exploration are more difficult to attain.

When a virtual team meeting is needed, management should provide training on the use and benefits of groupware technology. Management should also work with staff to set broad parameters for which occasions require groupware, interactive videoconferencing, or face-to-face sessions.

Technology permits each member of the virtual team to participate, but does become a filter through which the individual's ideas must pass. There is some degree of remove, or, less charitably, alienation that is felt when team membership and participation is mediated by equipment. It's important to recognize this syndrome so we can wrestle with the dysfunction that may occur as a result.

The challenge to making the virtual team work that is presented *by* technology can only be answered, in part, *with* technology. Technology by itself won't solve the problem. Staffs must employ basic teamwork strategies no matter where members are located; for instance, cross-functional teams located in a matrix need to follow the essential rules of effective matrix management. One of Strategic Futures's matrix success factors – role clarity – means, in part, defining the prerogatives of horizontal and vertical team leaders and members; it involves establishing the protocol for resolving dueling priorities and team members whether they are across the hall, across the street, or across the world.

The cybertrail of virtual team communications, coordination, project plans, interim products, etc., are all viewable by management if it tunes into the stream of e-mail traffic and other virtual communications. However, daily pressures seldom permit managerial monitoring of this kind. Furthermore, the inner workings of virtual teams are even more invisible to management than the workings of non-virtual teams that management can observe by happenstance.

Virtual Teams/Virtual Supervision

The upshot of management's relative lack of proximity to most virtual teams means that the virtual team leader and other participating functional supervisors need to monitor and sanction team member behavior with due diligence and care. The positive preservation and development of a team member's reputation, their "walking résumé," is a tremendous lever for monitoring and reinforcing peak performance and learning in a virtual environment where management's real leverage so often can be relatively faint or episodic at best.

Regardless of global location, it is essential that a shared-fate culture exist. In this culture, all members embrace a vision of collective success and share in its rewards. Effective project management becomes particularly critical, especially when a virtual team member participates on several teams, some virtual and some non-virtual. The classic features of excellent program and project management include clear, step-by-step work breakdown structures, and project timelines that are developed, communicated, and managed so that collisions between virtual and non-virtual team memberships are minimized. These steps guard against the disposing of virtual objectives, which may seem more expendable than their non-virtual counterparts just because of the power of face-to-face contact. It is one thing to be shunned in cyberspace and quite another to be shunned in person by the coworker who resides down the hall.

❑ **Among the Team Leader, Team Members, and Management**

As mentioned previously, the roles and rules that undergird the virtual matrix management team must be *even more* explicit than those that govern an in-house team. We need to be clear that the relationships are defined in such a way that support is given and support is received to get a job done. The ultimate authority for managing those relationships also must be spelled out clearly to keep cross-functional teams operating well in your virtual enterprise.

❑ **Among the Team Leader, Team Members, and Customers**

The CEO of a major, well-respected information technology company asked me once about the interface of a key customer located in Northern Virginia where a main functional element was located halfway across the country.

In one sense, there are functions and services that are quite appropriate for virtual team servicing: These functions and services are "backstage," invisible to the customer and, in that sense, can be performed anywhere. On the other hand, certain nuances – setting customer expectations, learning customer preferences, anticipating the customer requirements of tomorrow, forging a bond of trust that holds up in difficult times, and capturing a greater share of the wallet – are best understood and tracked through some degree of face time. When must the virtual team have a non-virtual appearance? When must the virtual bleed over into more traditional business dealings? My advice to the CEO was to ensure that the company arrange for regular, direct face time with the customer – either through the detailing and/or weekly fly-in of a key staff member so that there is a bonding with the customer. What's more, this temporary detail or fly-in person can be the human link between the customer and the virtual team members. All of this leads to the obvious conclusion that, despite the speed and cost-containment advantages of the virtual team, systematic human contact retains significant advantages that cannot be ignored.

❑ **Among Team Members**

One CEO offered his operational definition of "culture" – culture is how employees behave when the boss isn't around. Most of the work of virtual teams is, in fact, conducted without the boss looking. The virtual culture of your enterprise can only be as good as the overarching culture of your organization. In fact, those who participate on virtual teams are, to some extent, weaving a separate reality, a distinct culture where habits and traditions are in their earliest stage. Self-governance is the name of the game for most virtual teams. Members must develop rules that team members can adapt to individual project needs or to the idiosyncrasies presented by a given set of members. Team members who participate most actively and extensively on virtual teams may be able to play an oversight and coaching role that helps new virtual team members adapt. In this way, the values and norms of preferred team member behavior can be guided with a light touch rather than left to develop from the residue of a series of crisis-driven projects.

A Concluding Thought: Virtually Yours, Signed, Your Virtual Team

Virtual, cross-functional teams require a combined level of technological and organizational sophistication and a higher degree of emotional intelligence on the part of management and team members. It is unsafe to assume that technology can solve all of the virtual matrix team's challenges. Being "virtual" does not exempt the team from the roles and rules of matrix management. The principles of effective matrix management can and should be applied to smooth the functioning of all of your matrix teams.

CHAPTER 10:

Matrix Management in Government: *Goal-Directed Teams*

Matrix management is used by several government agencies, including by the Department of Defense's Department of the Navy and the Defense Finance and Accounting Service. The U.S. Geological Survey employed matrix management as part of a larger effort to achieve integrated science among hydrologists, geologists, geographers, and others. U.S. Food and Drug Administration --- Center for Devices and Radiological Health, and the Department of Health and Human Services' Substance Abuse and Mental Health Services Administration are other more recent examples.

There are numerous non-federal examples as well. One is the Fairfax County (Virginia) School System. Fairfax County Schools is the nation's 12th largest public school system and one of the nation's highest performing public school systems of any size. Several years ago, I used an extensive training campaign to help the county implement a matrix management system made up of 14 subdistrict geography-based matrix teams. These teams were chartered with the concept that the principals for the schools in their subdistrict were their customers. If these teams delivered for their principals, the principals would take care of the rest by ensuring student performance, parental involvement, and all of the other things that must be done school by school. Each matrix team was comprised of representatives from each of the many functions that it takes to make a school system work, such as curriculum, special education, transportation, facilities, human resources, technology, and more.

The example of matrix management that I believe best demonstrates its promise in government is at the U.S. National Oceanic and Atmospheric Administration (NOAA), where cross-cutting teams have been formed to pursue cross-cutting goals contained in the agency's strategic plan.

NOAA is comprised of several "Line Offices." The Line Office familiar to most Americans is the National Weather Service. Other, less familiar Line Offices include the National Ocean Service, the National Marine Fisheries Service, and the National Satellite Service for earth observation. One need not be a scientist to understand that the ocean affects the weather and that the fish swim in the sea, and that NOAA and its component parts would function well in a cross-cutting management structure. However, the formal NOAA organizational structure that Congress, constituent groups, the Office of Management and Budget, and others are accustomed to dealing with was forged some three decades ago. Needless to say, things have changed since then.

Changing a federal agency's organizational structure can be done through the legislative process, but presidential appointees temporarily heading these departments generally don't have time to dicker endlessly with the Congress about their proposals for organizational change. Such matters can gobble up half a decade and, even if success is attained, the sacrifices in employee morale or departures might be extremely damaging to the organization. To avoid this battle, the NOAA Administrator decided to update the agency's antiquated structure without Congress's "help." He identified several significant needs: (1) better use and development of NOAA's shared infrastructure of ships and aircraft; (2) integrated science; and (3) achievement of complex cross-cutting goals. He reasoned that he would need a structure that would encourage resource sharing and collaboration rather than one that would lead to internecine tugs of war for stovepipe budgets. He superimposed 20 goal-focused matrix teams across the traditional hierarchy for purposes of program planning, integration, budgeting, and program evaluation.

Are there still tugs of war? You bet. On the other hand, after several years of matrix management intended to achieve integrated program planning, budgeting, and program execution, there has been significant progress. For one thing, the planning and budgeting skirmishes today are of a higher quality! There are substantive issues being addressed that go beyond whose ox is being gored. The far-reaching consequences of funding or not funding activities and projects are now being examined more thoroughly and objectively. There are boundaries being spanned today that would not have been spanned before. Progress takes time, but early indications are that NOAA is successfully implementing matrix management.

Take the seemingly simple example of weather information for transportation planning. If cargo arrives by sea, and is then transferred to ground transport so that it can be shipped to its final destination by air, shippers need to know ocean weather, surface weather, and upper atmosphere weather. Customers want to know end-to-end weather patterns that will affect arrival commitments and other planning involved in product assembly, servicing, and more. That's three different sets of scientists and their data, not necessarily available in an integrated, let alone customized and customer-convenient, package. However, a cross-cutting matrix goal team can integrate the information and make it available to customers in a convenient format, facilitating safe and rapid commerce. The matrix team draws the pieces together through its oversight and by aligning strategy, systems, and service structures.

Special Challenges of Matrix Management in Government

The challenges to implementing matrix management in government are similar to those in private industry, but there are some special circumstances that warrant the brief discussion below.

1. **Performance appraisal systems in government** are often set in concrete, ruled by policy or regulation, statute, and/or collective-bargaining agreements. The performance appraisal of a matrix interface staff by two supervisors, vertical and horizontal, requires special adjustments. These adjustments involve constraining dimensions to be appraised by the vertical, or functional supervisor, and adding dimensions of appraisal to be performed by the horizontal matrix team leader. Consistent with the **Basic Matrix Role Dichotomy**, the functional leader will focus on appraising the performance of the matrixed employee relative to how the work got done and to what technical standard. The horizontal leader will focus largely on appraising performance along dimensions of how well the work got done, by what deadline and at what cost. This performance appraisal arrangement requires maturity on the part of the managers doing the evaluations so that they stay within their matrix boundaries and don't impose their perspectives in areas outside the bounds of their matrix management authority. This is especially complicated by situations where the vertical managers once had the horizontal matrix team leader's responsibilities and have had great difficulty "letting go." The human resources department needs to enforce the performance appraisal boundaries to avoid creating unworkable levels of confusion within the matrix.

2. **Oversight exercised by the legislative branch** is most often done on the basis of committees that deal with a particular part (stovepipe) of a particular public agency. This means that double-entry bookkeeping will be required so that financial planning and tracking can not only be accomplished for the horizontal matrix teams, but that it can be responsive to any and all oversight committees. I suggest that parallel systems be maintained, and that oversight bodies be apprised of the use of the matrix and shown both horizontal and vertical accounting.

3. **Public employee resistance to change is prevalent.** Large public bureaucracies respond slowly to change. It is important that the top career official make it clear that the matrix organization isn't going away, even with a change in administrations or congressional leadership on Capitol Hill. Middle management public employees may want to wait out a given political appointee and his or her ideas for change in the belief that the next appointee will reorganize and undo the matrix management structure. This lethargic response by employees can be avoided if the political appointee secures the top career executives' enthusiastic buy-in and then penetrates more deeply by winning the support of top management. With most top people on board with the plan, the notion that "this too shall pass" will diminish significantly, making change possible and even welcomed. Involving the career ranks actively in the move to matrix management is a powerful way to galvanize attention and lessen resistance throughout the agency.

A Concluding Thought

I have been doing consulting and training work in both the public and private sectors for more than a quarter century. Over the years, I have witnessed the differences between the two sectors diminish greatly when it comes to defining characteristics such as talented and hardworking staff, applications of technology, etc.

What has been slow to change in the public sector has been structure. Fossilized hierarchies abound in government but not just because of "bureaucrats." Congress' entrenched committee structures, stakeholder influence and pressures from invested constituents all combine together to cement obsolete structures into the fabric of the executive branch. As the NOAA example demonstrates, farsighted leaders are using matrix management to preserve structures insisted on by Congress and others, while at the same time achieving agility in the pursuit of cross-cutting goals using matrix management. It's evolving slowly. However, the good news is that developments are trending in the right direction.

CHAPTER 11:

Matrix Management in the IT Industry

A New Day for IT

It's a new day in the Information Technology world. Having weathered the Y2K threat, the dot.com-to-dot.bomb shakedowns and shakeouts, and all manner of mergers and breakups, it's time for executives, companies, and agencies to take a new look at the way in which they use technology to manage their enterprises.

In the IT world, the lack of a strategic or operational business plan is no longer "no problem." The easy access to Other People's Money, which fueled frenzied business practices, is no longer so forthcoming. Also in retreat is the "cult of personality," where the charismatic IT guru is encircled by a gaggle of sharp-elbowed techies that formed impenetrable spheres of influence. The "charismatic" insular era has given way to a more "rational" cooperative era.

The value of business planning and developing coherent business logic is becoming more widely appreciated in the industry. The idea that IT businesses should have a structural logic that holds together with a palpable center of gravity is gaining favor. This concept is beginning to gain greater favor in the IT departments of major corporations as well as in businesses that are strictly IT contractors.

Absent the center of gravity, an IT firm or, for that matter department, degrades into a mere bundle of projects where relationships among the projects and the personnel are largely accidental. Without synergy, how can there be growth? Without synergy, how can there be motivation and morale? Synergy is not an accident; it requires purposive planning and action. The structural logic of too many IT enterprises is more akin to a Persian rug market than it is to an ongoing, thriving enterprise with a long-range direction. Most of the randomly structured IT firms have joined the dearly departed. Randomly structured IT departments have seen turnover in top leadership. One result is that many of their projects in enterprises with traditions of disorganization have been outsourced to countries where the workforce requires lower levels of compensation and arguably possesses higher levels of motivation. If your company is not going to enjoy the benefits of organization and synergy when you are paying for it, why not cut your costs and ship the work to a job shop where frantic disorganization resulting in 15-hour days is the dominant order but saves you money – at least in the short run? (There are, of course, compromises to quality, which cost you money in the longer term, but if this is a top-of-mind concern, you are already convinced of this argument.)

Get Organized!

The astute IT companies are organizing to deliver value for their customers and profits and growth for themselves, and many recognize the value of matrix management in the pursuit of these goals. In the past year or so, I have worked with three IT companies that are distinguishing themselves.

One performs security-cleared projects for the U.S. government. This rapidly growing firm has moved to matrix teams organized by **customer** so that it can anticipate precisely customer needs, and build profits generated from existing and new customers. *Better value for the customer; better profitability and growth for the company.*

Another company that supplies top-notch bioinformatics and other computational services, with installations in the

United States and abroad, has organized matrix teams by **project** within defined **product** lines. *Better value for the customer; better profitability and growth for the company.*

Yet another company that provides automated systems for airlines is organized into a mix of matrix teams for **projects, product lines**, and **customers.** Multiple team assignments for key personnel achieve high productivity and synergy and gain sophisticated perspectives and insights. *Again, everybody wins.*

If it's worthwhile, it's probably not easy.

All of these companies faced matrix management implementation challenges. Some that were common to each enterprise are discussed below.

Shared Implementation Challenges

Help matrix team members leave their comfort zones. One shared challenge is helping matrix team members leave their comfort zones. This means that IT professionals who are not natural extroverts may need help with the "soft" skills, such as communications, persuasion, negotiation, and social assertiveness.

❑ Help matrix team members see new and different career patterns and opportunities. Another shared challenge is helping matrix team members see new and different career patterns and opportunities that are more freewheeling and lateral, and less about "hitching" to a particular IT star. Just as in cultures that rely more on relationships than on rules for getting things done, IT relationships can become paternalistic or protective and not lend themselves to a more cooperative, collaborative management structure. Whatever the source of frictional resistance to a more networked style of work organization, the changes associated with implementing a matrix structure need to be understood fully and addressed holistically – and with sensitivity to team members not used to this business style.

Clarify roles. IT projects appear to suffer from some common challenges with respect to role clarity. Here are some tips garnered from experience with matrixed IT project teams:

- ❑ Define roles and responsibilities, particularly Project Manager and Vertical Liaisons; have Vertical Liaisons involved in assigning project team players and ensure that there is *one* designated Project Manager

- ❑ Do more teambuilding up front as an IT team is commissioned

- ❑ Ensure mandatory participation of key players at selected points

- ❑ Create a project charter to define purpose and participation

- ❑ Do not plan with cavalier assumptions about *who* will ˙actually perform the work: Investigate and negotiate with certainty!

- ❑ If you are a Vertical Manager, select and train key players on your processes and procedures so that they can represent you in planning sessions. Focus on educating others so that they know how to get the best services out of your group

- ❑ Estimate correctly what it takes to on-board people onto a project with the active help of Vertical Liaisons

Define process clearly and precisely, which means:

- ❑ Stop pretending that each project is wholly unique and exempt from common core processes

- As roles, rules and tools are applied to a project, explain any and all adjustments to all parties
- Ensure that the Project Manager exercises authority to approach upper management for purposes of planning and securing resources .

Enhance staff interpersonal skills to:

- Provide timely and effective fact-based feedback to the right person(s)
- Work on ownership issues and boundary issues to achieve clarity
- Conduct meetings with a defined agenda, with the right people – not too many and not too few – with written minutes

Ensure that principles of effective management – matrix and otherwise – are observed throughout to:

- Align project objectives so that desired outcomes can be attained
- Identify project expectations explicitly at the beginning of the project
- Identify timing for the involvement of vertical functions when their involvement is called for – not too late, but not too early either and require that the right people be involved rather than always requiring everyone to be involved all of the time
- Engage leadership in setting and approving realistic financial requirements at the beginning of the project
- Flow diagram the project from beginning to end
- Secure and cultivate buy-in from people throughout – not just at the beginning but through a process of "continuous selling"

- Give project participants input – use collaboration rather than dictation

- Use a matrix management approach that focuses on outcomes, rather than attempting to micro-manage activity and approach

- Promote a shared-fate culture rather than relying on fear-based management.

A Concluding Thought

Matrix management is used frequently in performing IT projects both in IT firms and in IT departments. To the extent that poor project management practices are used, matrix management can only enjoy limited success. It is not unusual for an enterprise to engage in sloppy project management and then blame resulting problems on matrix management. A closer inspection and more precise diagnosis of problems reveal that the use of matrix management for accomplishing multiple IT projects requires not only that the principles of effective matrix management be observed but also the principles of effective project management.

CHAPTER 12:

Matrix Management and Integrated Selling

Matrix management has now organized your business by aligning the tasks, goals, and outcomes of your disparate branches, offices, or agencies, and provided a cross-cutting framework to manage the entire enterprise. Now you'll want to use matrix management to maximize product sales using integrated selling.

But what is integrated selling? For the "feet-on-the-street" sales force, it means selling a product/service that is outside the comfort zone or beyond the perceived "control" of the sales representative. Top management wants to conduct integrated selling to create a cascade of additional sales of new products and services to existing customers, which avoids the clumsy embarrassments, selling expenses, and opportunity costs associated with Company Representative 1 showing up on Tuesday to sell Product A and Company Sales Representative 2 showing up on Thursday to sell Product B. The benefits of integrated selling should provide the following results.

- ❏ Increased gross revenue and profitability

- ❏ Increased focus on customer wants and needs rather than focus on "selling" a product or service

- ❏ Synergy among products and services that increases market and wallet share

- ❏ Minimized instances of the sales force working at cross-purposes

- ❏ Minimized sales clumsiness, duplication, expenses, and opportunity costs

Sounds good conceptually, doesn't it? So why not just snap your fingers and make it happen? The problem in taking integrated selling from elegant concept to actual fruition is that the sales representative will need to get beyond good intentions, let go of past habits and beliefs, and make it happen.

For the sales representative, this means trusting others in the company who are "unknowns" or "wild cards" as the sales force moves to team-based selling. It means opening doors to unfamiliar product and service sets where the sales person can't necessarily answer the customer's questions or objections in a personal and immediate way. It means seeing new possibilities beyond the familiar.

For example, if you have a long career history of selling oral hygiene products to grocery and drug store chains, collaborating with your colleagues who sell smoking-cessation products, stomach-indigestion products, and over-the-counter pain-relief medications will take you to new places. To cite another example, where you once just sold refrigeration units for storing and displaying products in existing grocery stores, now, using integrated selling, you collaborate with people selling refrigeration units for the trucks that move the products and you collaborate with new grocery store construction designers. You also sell aftermarket vendor service contracts for every product that your company sells.

Conceptually, it's easy to see that integrated selling can not only provide greater levels of convenience to your business client, but also can breathe life into the often theoretical idea that "we should be cross-selling all of our products and services everywhere." However, as with everything related to matrix management, the rub is in taking things from chic concept to the rough and tumble of daily implementation.

Indeed, there's a whole lot of "letting go" that is involved with a move from individual "cowboy" selling towards integrated selling. What does the sales representative perceive he or she is giving up in moving from individual sales to team-based integrated selling?

- The large degree of influence-bordering-on-control that a sales representative has cultivated with contacts in the customer organization around a particular product/service;

- The comfort that comes from dealing with familiar individuals, rather than greeting new faces, typically higher-ranking individuals in the customer organization who need to be approached with comprehensive solutions, or for larger orders or anything remotely novel;

- The sense of confidence from knowing a product/service inside and out and the people who make and/or deliver the product/service, and from a deep sense of why, how, and when the customer buys (a new product/service could upset the apple cart of predictable sales);

- A clear answer to "who made the sale?" and resultant concerns about compensation;

- The freedom of movement that independent selling provides – a flexibility that seems to be diminished by the coordinated schedules of team-based selling;

- A sense of ego or security that comes from being the "golden connection" that links the customer with a product/service.

If you want to ensure that integrated selling catches fire, the concerns of the sales force as bulleted above, along with other concerns that may exist at your particular company, must be addressed head-on. It is essential that solutions be developed with the active participation of key sales representatives, particularly those who are most respected and influential.

There are no "one-size-fits-all" steps to moving to integrated selling. However, one useful generalization can be offered: All-or-nothing thinking on any of these issues will take you places that you do not want to go. For instance, there is little value in arrangements where your key representative to a client says, "We've had some changes and I won't be seeing you much anymore ... if at all."

Integrated selling teams should, to the fullest extent possible, be configured so that all prior customer contacts are maintained and that these contacts introduce their colleagues as additional resources to the customer's personnel. Integrated selling becomes more a matter of organized "swarming" of the customer with the team members rather than a matter of replacing one individual sales representative with another person.

A few years ago, I worked with a manufacturing client that adopted an integrated selling approach. This company had the most marvelous sales force that I have ever seen. They were fully professional, yet friendly, if not downright jovial. They were all making good money and enjoyed what they were doing and with whom they were doing it. They were "experimentalists," sufficiently secure in their competency and relationships that the prospect of integrated selling – *with the real possibility of higher earnings for each of them using the matrixed approach* – was stirring and exciting.

I asked the Vice President for human resources whether he had administered pre-hiring psychological tests to this sales force to achieve the degree of interpersonal harmony that was apparent to anyone who looked. He laughed and said, "I wish." He explained that it was really more a matter of careful hiring to ensure that each member would be a good fit with what I can only call a "Zen sales culture." By Zen sales culture, I mean my imperfect definition of a tremendous environment that was hard driving in its performance focus, but easygoing and friendly by way of mutual support, both within management and among peers. This established culture had been nurtured over a century by each succeeding generation of managers. Add a little bit of good luck and stir to achieve a remarkably positive organization unencumbered by pretense and unafraid of change.

If you are moving to integrated selling, you need to take a clear-eyed look at your sales culture. If you have a somewhat combative individualistic culture, you will need to do a greater amount of preparatory work in getting your organization ready for a new way of doing business. If this step is needed, you can't skip it.

A Concluding Thought

An integrated selling strategy that is unaccompanied by corresponding realignments of systems and structure will remain a chic concept that receives lip service and little else. The matrix organization is a natural fit with the integrated selling strategy, but it is somewhat "counterintuitive" to a sales "cowboy" who is probably accustomed to working solo. Integrated selling using a matrix organization works! However, extraordinary efforts to prepare the sales force for this change are almost certainly required. It's an investment well worth making.

CHAPTER 13:

Matrix Management and Beyond – *Emerging Organizational Architecture*

As we say at our firm, Strategic Futures®, the strategic future is now! The strategic future flows from today's thoughtful decisions, investments, and actions. As we gaze into our proverbial crystal ball, let's look at some of the exciting possibilities that may stem from the successful matrix organization.

The Multi-Organization Matrix. You can form a multi-organization matrix as a byproduct of a strategic alliance or partnership among two or more organizations whose staff are collaborating in well-structured, results-oriented projects. As the boundaries among cooperating organizations blur, staff from various organizations cooperate on teams and "shed" a bit of the identity of their employing organization as they acquire the identity of the matrix team of which they have become a member.

Now if you thought that standing up a matrix in your own organization was an enormous task, consider linking a strategic partner or two to extend the functional capabilities of the matrix team. The deployment of a multi-organization matrix makes a critical assumption, namely that the participating organizations are more or less on the same page when it comes to matrix management – conceptually and by way of roles, rules, and staff capabilities. However, beware the old saying about "assume" – the one about making an "ass" out of both "u" and "me" – and refrain from cobbling together multiple organizations into a multi-organizational matrix without deliberate and explicit fact-finding and matrix team development.

The Instant Matrix. The "instant matrix" will become more common as organizations come to use matrix management more routinely and with a relatively stable and uniform set of definitions and rules of engagement. Matrix structures are likely to become increasingly flexible and dynamic. The use of temporary matrix structures, availability of specialized capabilities defined in person-hours, displays of work process, and employment of up-to-the-minute performance metrics will become the rule rather than the exception. Multiple matrix teams in various states of creation, operation, and dismantling will coexist. In fact, multiple matrices are likely to coexist as temporary constructs.

The Layered Matrix. When a matrix develops within a matrix, we have the seeds of trouble. I have visited any number of organizations that delighted in telling me that they have a matrix (or two) within a matrix and reveled in the complexity of it all.

We should walk before we run when it comes to matrix management. Use of the layered matrix should be reserved to the virtuoso class because the perils of confusing everyone are too great.

When would we use a layered matrix? External developments or internal breakthroughs may so magnify the functional importance of a particular matrix interface that it needs to be supercharged and expanded radically to proceed. This "all-hands-on-deck" imperative may require deployment of a specialized team-within-a-team to support the matrix interface on an expanded and/or expedited level.

The need for "hyperstaffing" gives rise to the layered matrix. Expanded teams may be drawn from other matrix interfaces, from outside of the matrix, and/or from outside vendors. The key to success in using matrix management in this dynamic way is that participating staff are pre-trained and exercised so that they know where to go, what to do, and how to relate to one another and to other participants in the organization – whether the other staffs are "inside" or "outside" of the matrix.

These types of *ad hoc* arrangements are fast, daring, and exciting, but adequate preparation spells the difference between success and failure.

A Final Word

I never try to sell anyone on matrix management as a structural strategy; people must reach their own conclusions about the need for change of this significance. When employees in an organization find themselves out of breath on an unceasing basis, they will agitate for change, if the leaders don't. Exhaustion with the old way of doing things builds the sense of urgency that fuels the effort to plan for and implement matrix management.

Ultimately, the best litmus test of whether matrix management is working is to ask people if they find it easier to use the matrix to get their work done and be successful or whether they find it easier to "go around" the matrix organization to conduct their daily affairs.

If we have done a good job of designing and implementing the matrix organization, people will embrace it rather than bypass it. When that happens, your enterprise will be faster, more agile, and better able to pursue goals and manage complexity – and will be well positioned to compete with the hierarchical and/or disorganized dinosaurs. You can do it if you think before you speak and plan before you act: Adopt a methodical approach of ready-aim-fire and you will find success with matrix management!

AFTERWORD: NEW FRONTIERS

Take a close look at an effective leader and you will often see an individual who not only knows how to jump out in front of a parade and assume the role of parade master, but also works behind the scenes to organize all of the constituencies that will be marching in the parade to step out smartly. This leader shares a vision, builds excitement and motivation, gets understanding and buy-in for strategies and tactics … and so much more.

As we know, the leader who jumps to the head of the parade without doing the behind-the-scenes work usually doesn't last long, or if s/he does, people often wish them gone. Why? To recall this book's subtitle, such a leader relies on magic rather than method among other things.

The ancient magic of summarily issuing an order which will be implemented unquestioningly by staff seems to have all but disappeared in many places – apart from the military where an uncompromised authority is, of course, vital. Without judging this apparent "breakdown" of traditional authority in non-military organizations to be either good or bad, it does seem to be prevalent. Why? That's a book unto itself and a fascinating one at that. I personally believe that the shift away from formal authority has been hastened by the ubiquity of information. However, less obvious variables have undoubtedly had impact; for example, in the dot.com era, some leaders learned the hard way that it's plenty tough to exercise formal authority over someone who had raised more venture capital for the company than you had! The dot.com era made this phenomenon more visible but this is a situation that has existed both before and after dot.com/dot.bomb.

Whatever the explanation, leadership today has as much to do with the exercise of influence than it does with the wielding of traditional power. (The exception to this trend is the leader who surrounds himself with unquestioning "yes men" who accept gladly whatever orders may issue forth, but we digress.)

Looking away from the past and towards the future, leadership of and in the ideal matrix organization is "holographic." By this I mean that each subordinate leader in the matrix, meaning horizontal and vertical leaders as well as staff interface liaisons, is a "chip off the old block" – an expression of the top leader's grand direction, function by function, team by team. This expression is reflective rather than robotic. Leadership behavior and leadership themes are penetrated more deeply into the enterprise using matrix management – or at least they should be.

However, to make the ideal become real – to achieve full potential – staff need to master the competencies necessary for success. There are lots of great books about leadership, leadership behaviors, competencies, metrics and the like. I will not assault the forest, wasting paper to paraphrase these or cite them *ad nauseam*.

On the other hand, I believe that the next frontier for furthering matrix management success entails meticulous definition of "soft skills" -- which are needed to help people on cross-functional teams with multiple obligations collaborate more smoothly -- even in the face of chronic resource challenges.

There is an array of "soft skills" needed for success in a matrix organization. If these soft skills are relatively scarce among your colleagues, don't panic. This is not a show-stopper. Interpersonal skills and human relations can improve of their own accord and they often do. However, make no mistake that success comes more easily to organizations that are staffed with people who communicate readily and easily, persuade, negotiate, and otherwise problem-solve together. Training and development can grow these soft skills faster and better, and with fewer sacrifices of productivity *ergo* profitability.

We have established that getting things done in a matrix organization requires the exercise of influence, more often than not with little or no authority. Folks in a traditional hierarchy may rightfully ask, "what else is new?" given that the exercise of authority can be diffuse, if not downright confused in a traditional organization. Be that as it may, our expectations of the matrix organization are higher! Our focus is on the challenge presented to players in the *matrix* arena and as such, the exercise of influence with little or no authority is a core competency for vertical leaders, horizontal team leaders, and functional liaison go-to people alike.

We have also established that the functional liaisons who are members of the horizontal team are people who will make or break your matrix organization. To the extent that they have the soft skills needed to know when and how to convince others to, e.g., commit to action; give others stake in the action; or create enthusiasm for the action, as well as other competencies needed to have effective relations "outside the formal chain of command," the performance of your enterprise can improve appreciably.

These soft skills include core competencies needed to overcome personal issues that get in the way of resolving problems with colleagues. They include the ability to figure out who needs to be led and knowing where there will be resistance and why. With all of this, the name of the game is to resolve as many of the sticky issues within the matrix structure itself – resorting to more forceful methods or appeals to higher authority less frequently over time.

As "soft skill" competency both deepens and broadens in your organization, it stands to reason that the job satisfaction of your people can increase. As time progresses, there will be greater comfort, convenience, and yes, success, found in "using the matrix" rather than in "by-passing" it as staff skills become more closely aligned with requirements of the matrix structure.

Furtherance of the soft skills required for matrix management success is where we're headed next. Hope to see you there!

.

GLOSSARY OF TERMS

Basic Matrix Role Dichotomy – The cornerstone of matrix management and the basis for clarifying horizontal and vertical roles. The Basic Matrix Role Dichotomy defines the responsibilities and prerogatives of the Vertical Manager and the Horizontal Manager.

Capability – The assortment of talent, money and infrastructure needed to perform a core competency of the organization that is necessary to its successful delivery of value.

Capacity – The amount or magnitude of a capability that is readily available for use.

Charter – A charter defines what a matrix team is in business to do, why it is doing it and how it supposed to do it, with emphasis on the advantages of cross-functional collaboration and the use of shared resources towards accomplishment of a shared goal.

Complex Tension – An unhealthy tension which arises when there are unresolved issues among different functions and different teams in the matrix; these tensions may arise from objectives being out of alignment, strife concerning scarce resources, lack of role clarity, lack of process clarity and the like.

Constructive Tension – A healthy tension which exists among the vertical and horizontal components of a matrix organization, which results in the eradication of unnecessary work or work that adds sufficient value to goal accomplishment and/or customer satisfaction, the full utilization of organizational capabilities and capacities, and a goal-focus that heightens sense of urgency, productivity, and performance in the enterprise.

Darwinian Management – A phrase used to describe a practice of launching more projects and initiatives than an organization can hope to achieve within its existing capabilities and capacities with the usually unspoken strategy of weeding out those projects or initiatives that lack clear objectives, can't garner sufficient internal support and/or can't muster the resources necessary for their successful execution.

Drive-By Reorganization™ – A phrase used to describe a relatively unorganized, even haphazard approach to structural change in the organization, usually accompanied by incomplete or unclear definitions of who is supposed to do what differently and to what end.

Horizontal Manager – A manager who is in charge of a horizontal matrix team, ultimately responsible for deciding questions concerning what is to be done, when it is to be done, why it is to be done, and how much money is available to do it. The horizontal manager is also responsible for assessing how well the total effort has been done. S/he is responsible for providing personnel appraisal input for those team members who have contributed significantly to matrix team performance. The *proviso* for such input is that it be restricted to issues that are within the Horizontal Manager's purview, e.g., what is to be done, when, why, and by way of resource coordination and contributions to the overall end result.

Interface – This term describes the key individuals who are drawn from functions which are participating on a horizontal matrix team. Also called staff interface, and vertical liaison, this team player reports to both the Horizontal Manager and the Vertical Manager in accordance with the Basic Matrix Role Dichotomy.

Interfunction Tension – An unhealthy tension that exists among vertical functions of a matrix, usually related to unexpected delays in performance by one function which upsets the plans for staff deployment of another function. This tension can also occur when boundaries between functions are blurred or when there are conflicting functional objectives that are creating controversy or dueling priorities among functions.

Interteam Tension – An unhealthy tension that exists among matrix teams usually associated with a "resource stockout," meaning that both teams seek to share resources at the same time for which there is inadequate capability, capacity, or both.

LACI – A format and process for interrogating through the steps in a defined process, asking questions concerning the contribution made by each of the roles towards making decisions and performing work. LACI is an acronym which stands for **L**ead, **A**pprove, **C**onsult, and **I**nform. The technique was originally developed in engineering environments. An alternate method is RACI, where R stands for **R**esponsibility. A hybrid version RLACI permits definition using the LACI terminology plus the pinpointed identification of a function expected to perform work once a decision has been made.

Matrix Management – An approach to management which cobbles together a battery of cross-functional teams which are using shared resources to pursue shared objectives under leadership that is both horizontal and vertical.

Matrix Management Success Leadership Model – A construct developed by Strategic Futures Consulting Group, Inc. which defines the characteristics that are essential to matrix management success. These characteristics include role clarity, process definition, objectives alignment, resource alignment, shared-fate culture, matrix-friendly systems, e.g., HR and financial management, staff confidence, and staff interpersonal skills.

Vertical Leader – The leader of a function or discipline in the organization which operates as a "store" that matrix teams draw upon for the performance of their charter. The vertical function supplies personnel and defines how and where tasks will be done. The Vertical Leader assesses how well the input of his/her function has been integrated into the efforts of the cross-functional matrix team.

Vertical Liaison – See interface above.

BIBLIOGRAPHY

Barnes, Kim B., *Exercising Influence.* Berkeley: Barnes and Conti Associates, 2000.

Berger, Peter L. and Luckmann, Thomas. *The Social Construction of Reality.* Garden City: Doubleday Anchor, 1966.

Bradford, David L., and Cohen, Allan R., *Influence Without Authority.* Hoboken: John Wiley & Sons, 2005.

Cameron, Kim S. and Quinn, Robert E., *Diagnosing and Changing Organizational Culture.* Menlo Park: Addison-Wesley, 1999.

Cleland, David I., *Strategic Management of Teams.* New York: John Wiley & Sons, 1996.

Donnellon, Anne, *Team Talk.* Boston: Harvard Business School Press, 1996.

Goffman, Erving, *Asylums.* Garden City: Doubleday Anchor, 1961.

Kotter, John P., *Leading Change.* Boston: Harvard Business School Press, 1996.

Kotter, John P., *Power and Influence: Beyond Formal Authority.* New York: The Free Press, 1985.

Lipnack, Jessica and Stamps, Jeffrey. *Virtual Teams: People Working Across Boundaries with Technology.* New York: John Wiley & Sons, 2000.

Parker, Glenn M., *Cross-Functional Teams: Working with Allies, Enemies and Other Strangers.* San Francisco: Jossey-Bass, 1994.

Stacey, Ralph D., *Managing the Unknowable: Strategic Boundaries Between Order and Chaos in Organizations.* San Francisco: Jossey-Bass, 1992.